Racial
Wellness

A Guide to Liberatory Healing
for Black, Indigenous, and People of Color

JACQUELYN OGORCHUKWU IYAMAH

Clarkson Potter/Publishers
New York

Published in the United States by Clarkson Potter/Publishers, an
imprint of the Crown Publishing Group, a division of Penguin Random
House LLC, New York.
ClarksonPotter.com

CLARKSON POTTER is a trademark and POTTER with colophon
is a registered trademark of Penguin Random House LLC.

ISBN 978-0-593-57935-0
eISBN 978-0-593-57936-7

Printed in China

Diagrams by Jacquelyn Ogorchukwu Iyamah and Jan Derevjanek

10 9 8 7 6 5 4 3 2 1

First Edition

Contents

A Shared Language

Before we begin, it is important that we all have a shared language.

BIPOC	*BIPOC* is an acronym for Black, Indigenous, and people of color. This term is used to ensure that we remember Black and Indigenous peoples who have faced extreme erasure by the term *people of color*.
Latine	*Latine* is a gender-neutral term for Latino and Latina. The term has been said to integrate more seamlessly than the term *Latinx* into the Spanish language due to the "e" ending. However, it is important to note that there is no consensus on which term to use.
White Supremacist Culture	*White supremacist culture* speaks to the beliefs, values, norms, and practices that covertly and overtly perpetuate the ideology that white people are superior to Black, Indigenous, and people of color. By defining white people as superior, white supremacist culture justifies the ways in which white people oppress communities of color to dominate them politically, economically, and socially.
Racism	*Racism* is a system of abuse that oppresses Black, Indigenous, and people of color on structural, institutional, interpersonal, and internalized levels. Racism involves one group having the singular power to carry out systematic racial oppression through policies, programs, and practices.
Racial Trauma	*Racial trauma* consists of the ongoing and wide-ranging wounds that Black, Indigenous, and people of color experience because of white supremacy and racism.
Racial Wellness	*Racial wellness* speaks to the practices we weave into our lives to tend to the emotional, mental, physical, and spiritual effects that white supremacy and racism have on our well-being.

Prelude

My first memories of racism were with my white kindergarten teachers in France. At such a young age, I was unable to comprehend why my teachers treated my white peers with tenderness and me with callousness. And while I was not aware of what racism was at that age, I understood that the biggest difference between me and my peers was the color of our skin.

As I grew older, I began to understand how pervasive anti-Blackness was. I began to observe, recognize, and dissect the harm that I was facing. Still, I never felt like I had the space to fully express what I was experiencing. It wasn't until I moved to the United States in 2012 to start my undergraduate degree in social welfare that I began to find spaces that gave me the tools to talk not only about racism but also about how it impacts Black, Indigenous, and people of color.

Years of research have explored the role of racism on our mental health. The work to highlight racial trauma was led by experts such as the psychologist Robert T. Carter, the psychologist Thema Bryant, and the researcher Joy DeGruy. I had the honor of serving as a consultant on *Skindeep* (2021), a film about race-based trauma, with Carter, whose work set in motion the conversation about racial trauma in the field of psychology. Carter first used the term *race-based traumatic stress* in his 2007 paper "Racism and Psychological and Emotional Injury: Recognizing and Assessing Race-Based Traumatic Stress."

I call racism "the multifaceted abuser" because it abuses our communities emotionally, mentally, physically, and spiritually. When we practice reframing "racism" as "abuse" and "racist" as "abusive," we get a clearer image of the impact racism has on people. Unfortunately, as a society and in psychology, we rarely frame racism as a form of abuse. The cognitive dissonance is so deep that people are often confused when they see the words *racism* and *abuse* woven together. This has resulted in a lack of care for Black, Indigenous, and people of color who experience racism.

Take, for example, the therapists who know how to help people who have experienced other types of abuse but who are not equipped to help people of color navigate racial trauma. Or the employers who expect people of color to sit through the same antiracism workshops as white people, when, in *any* abusive dynamic, the person benefiting from the abuse and the person experiencing the abuse need vastly different things. Or even the white people who casually bring up racist events without thinking to use sensitivity warnings in the same ways they would with other forms of abuse.

As someone who has always been passionate about using creativity as a portal to liberation, I was curious if there were ways for me to use design to stimulate healing for communities of color. In 2018, I began my graduate degree in interaction design. I spent time conducting research into how to design spaces that provide soft landings for those dealing with racial trauma. I tapped into theory from my social welfare degree, praxis from my design degree, and wisdom from my loving ancestors to reimagine the ways in which racial healing can take place. I concluded that these spaces need to be accessible, educational, and led by people with lived experience.

I began to create a space on Instagram where I design healing-informed graphics that help people to understand, reflect, and cope with racial trauma. This work provided a tender space for Black, Indigenous, and people of color during the racial unrest in the summer of 2020. Then, in August 2020, I launched Making the Body a Home, a platform that stimulates racial wellness through intentional homeware products and educational course offerings. Since then, my practice of using design to promote racial wellness has touched people in tangible ways.

Today, the community of people who resonate with my work has grown to tens of thousands. This community is filled with people from all walks of life: students, therapists, parents, teachers, and more who share how transformational this work has been for them. These paradigm shifts, along with the work of other visionaries I deeply admire, have played a beautiful role in setting the conversation about racial wellness in motion on a large scale. In November 2020, the American Medical Association finally recognized racism as a threat to public health. In October 2021, the American Psychological Association apologized for its perpetuation of racism and inaction in not recognizing racial trauma.

This book is a tender continuation of this work. As someone who is inspired by the infographics about Black America created by W. E. B. Du Bois and his students, I've always longed for a design-forward book with offerings that help Black, Indigenous, and people of color to rest, rehabilitate, and rebuild. There is so much power that can be found in design. The role of visual culture in racial liberation cannot be overlooked.

Interlude

Racial trauma consists of the ongoing and wide-ranging wounds that Black, Indigenous, and people of color experience because of racism. Global forms of racial abuse such as colonization, genocide, and slavery have contributed to the widespread perpetuation of racism on institutional, interpersonal, and internalized levels.

INSTITUTIONAL RACIAL TRAUMA is caused by unfair policies and practices within and by institutions that produce inequitable outcomes for Black, Indigenous, and people of color. Here are some examples:

Racist policing practices
Racially biased hiring practices
Racially biased healthcare treatment
Racist policies, programs, and practices in schools
Lack of BIPOC representation in the media

INTERPERSONAL RACIAL TRAUMA is caused by individuals who project degrading thoughts, beliefs, and behaviors toward Black, Indigenous, and people of color. This includes the following:

Racial stereotypes
Racial hate crimes
Racial bullying
Racial slurs and hate speech
Racial dignity assaults (microaggressions)

INTERNALIZED RACIAL TRAUMA speaks to the ways in which Black, Indigenous, and people of color may internalize the harmful messaging that we are inferior. In any abusive dynamic, it is common for the victim to have a diminished sense of self. This is what it looks like:

Feeling racial inferiority and shame
Perpetuating harmful stereotypes about your community
Conforming to white beauty standards
Idealizing white values, practices, and culture
Distancing yourself from your community

When we are exposed to trauma and loss in these intricate ways, we experience *racial grief*. It can be difficult to navigate racial grief because racism is constant, permeating our everyday lives. Justin Grinage, a professor whose work explores racial loss and grief, refers to this experience as "an endless mourning." He shares, "Within this framework, the individual or group experiencing racial trauma cannot hope to entirely shed themselves of this trauma, since new traumas emerge and accumulate."

We're often taught that not being able to "move on" from this pain is a sign of personal failure. I've learned that this couldn't be further from the truth. Not being able to adjust to racial trauma is a sign of our humanity. It is a sign that we are not desensitized. It is a sign that our hearts know that we deserve better. The truth is that it would be difficult for anyone to exist without grief within a system that was not designed to support them.

Racial trauma and loss can impact us and manifest in several ways:

EMOTIONALLY: Depression, anger, rage, and sadness
MENTALLY: Anxiety, confusion, chronic stress, and dissociation
PHYSICALLY: Fatigue, illness, hypervigilance, and inflammation
SPIRITUALLY: Internalized racial inferiority, shame, low self-worth, and loss of identity

To navigate this continuous trauma and loss, we must create space and time to tend to ourselves. In the following pages, we will explore how you can care for your emotional, mental, physical, and spiritual well-being in the face of racism. Each section allows you space to explore your trauma through reflection prompts, affirmations, and tender reminders, and offers you guidance on your healing journey on individual, interpersonal, and institutional levels.

Oftentimes when we try to treat trauma, we are not multidimensional in our approach. We focus on the individual but not on the institutional factors that may have caused harm to that person in the first place. This approach can make us feel like we are to blame for trauma caused by oppression. The reality is that inner work alone cannot save us from experiencing racial wounds. This is not to say that practices such as individual therapy cannot be helpful in the face of racial trauma; it simply means we must be intentional with the type of support we seek. Therapists, support groups, or healing circles that are centered on anti-oppressive, decolonized racial healing can be transformational. Racism takes place on different levels in society, and thus our healing practices must acknowledge this.

May this book stimulate a revolutionary paradigm of care for you, me, and us.

Emotional Wellness

The following chapters
explore how racism impacts
our hearts, and provide
guidance on how we make
room for our humanity.

You deserve to show up in this world.

Honoring
Your Hurt

EXPLORING RACIAL APATHY

Racial apathy is a form of emotional neglect toward Black, Indigenous, and people of color rooted in the biased belief that we do not feel pain. As white supremacist culture weaves together narratives that white people are fragile and soft while communities of color are resilient and harsh, it births a hostile environment that does not care for us in the ways that we deserve.

The ways in which these narratives thread through our lives are devastating. Studies show that white people often feel more empathy when other white people experience pain and significantly less empathy when Black people experience pain; the treatment of BIPOC immigrants, refugees, and asylum seekers is worse than the treatment of white people in the same circumstances. And responses to natural disasters are often slower or nonexistent in areas where the victims are predominantly Black or brown than where they are white.

Dehumanization is the reason why racial apathy is so persistent. When you define someone as a "lesser human," it is *easier* to desensitize yourself to their inherent tenderness and become apathetic toward them and their painful experiences—including with racism. It is for these reasons that society often prioritizes white people's comfort over our pain.

When I was in middle school, a white student said something racist toward me, and our teacher consoled the student (who was upset that I told them off) instead of consoling me (the person who experienced the harm). In a moment when I deeply needed care, whiteness was the priority. I learned very quickly that I was navigating an environment where my feelings came second to white people's feelings. Professor Megan Boler describes this unequal emotional dynamic as *feeling power*. In essence, the feelings of those in power take precedence and are normalized over the feelings of those who are oppressed.

RACIAL APATHY

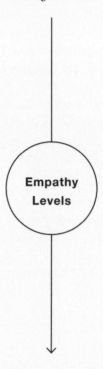

*White people and people
with lighter skin*

**Empathy
Levels**

*BIPOC and people
with darker skin*

HOW RACIAL APATHY MANIFESTS

Racial apathy manifests as people minimizing and disregarding the emotional needs of Black, Indigenous, and people of color. It often involves a lack of interest, emotion, and motivation to act.

Here's what racial apathy can look like:

LACK OF INTEREST

Disengagement	Tuning out of conversations about racism *People get bored, change the subject, sigh, or roll their eyes when BIPOC talk about racism.*
Maintaining normalcy	Operating in a "business as usual" mode when BIPOC have experienced racism *Employers fail to address or condemn widely publicized racist events.*
Neutrality	Choosing to be detached from issues that harm BIPOC *People label themselves as "apolitical" when it comes to issues of racial oppression.*

LACK OF EMOTION

Insensitivity	Feeling unmoved when witnessing BIPOC express sadness or hurt *People criticize BIPOC for being vulnerable about racism and tell us to "get over" it.*
Dehumanization	Viewing white people as more human and thus capable of more feeling than BIPOC *Doctors often believe that Black people have a higher pain tolerance than white people.*

| Selective empathy | Showing empathy only when white people experience hardship |
| | *The media view wars, disasters, and viruses in predominantly white areas as more worthy of public attention and media coverage than those affecting areas where BIPOC predominantly reside.* |

LACK OF MOTIVATION TO ACT

| Nonparticipation | Demonstrating no motivation to participate in causes that support BIPOC |
| | *People lack the motivation to join protests or mobilizations against racial oppression.* |

| Bystander apathy | Failing to intervene and defend BIPOC who are experiencing racism |
| | *People choose to not intervene when they see a Black person experiencing anti-Blackness.* |

| Neglect | Not paying attention to or acting on the hardships that BIPOC experience |
| | *Police neglect Black and Indigenous women's missing-person reports.* |

THE IMPACT OF RACIAL APATHY

Here are some of the ways selective racial empathy can impact you:

- It can cause you to minimize, reject, or numb your own feelings.
- It can make you feel like your racialized pain does not matter.
- It can make you feel like it isn't safe to voice your hurt and needs.
- It can make you feel like white people's experiences are more important than yours.
- It can make it difficult for you to be vulnerable with others and form intimate relationships.

When we are consistently held to unrelenting standards during hardships, treated as if we are a low priority, and shown that our emotional needs are insignificant, we quickly start to feel that it is unsafe for us to express our hurt. Emotional neglect can cause many of us to believe that we are not deserving of people who can hold our stories with warmth. My wish is that we get to experience genuine care in response to any form of harm we deal with so that we can process heavy emotions. We are not meant to swallow our hurt.

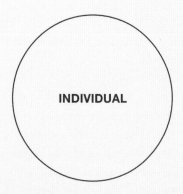

INDIVIDUAL

**HOW TO TEND
TO YOURSELF**

Feel Your Feelings

In a world that tries to deny your ability to feel, taking the time to hold space for your hurt is a radical act. You can do the following:

- Give yourself permission to talk, cry, and journal about it.
- Create art. Art is a powerful tool that helps us express, understand, and validate our emotions.
- Join in-person or online BIPOC support groups that allow you to connect with people who center your experiences.

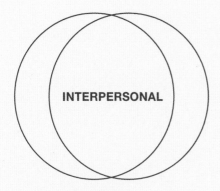

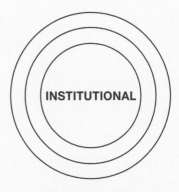

Protect Your Humanity

Practice affirming your humanity when you are around people who are racially apathetic. You can do the following:

- Don't spend energy trying to make someone have empathy for you. Walk away from people who make you feel like you have to prove your humanity.
- Remember that someone's inability to see the full humanity of BIPOC is not a reflection of your lack of humanity; it's a reflection of theirs.
- Cultivate relationships with friends, family, or community who know how to hold space for your hurt and fight for you.

Promote Racial Empathy

Advocate for genuine interest, emotion, and care toward Black, Indigenous, and people of color. You can do the following:

- Condemn selective racial empathy when you see it taking place in the media—which influences what we are taught to care about. This puts pressure on society at large to confront the ways in which they neglect BIPOC.
- Amplify the need for widespread rehumanization initiatives. Rehumanization is a process of rejecting identity-based hierarchies such as racial hierarchies from our hearts. This type of transformational work may help people see the humanity in BIPOC and embody racial empathy.

Reflection

Take a moment to explore how racial apathy makes you feel.

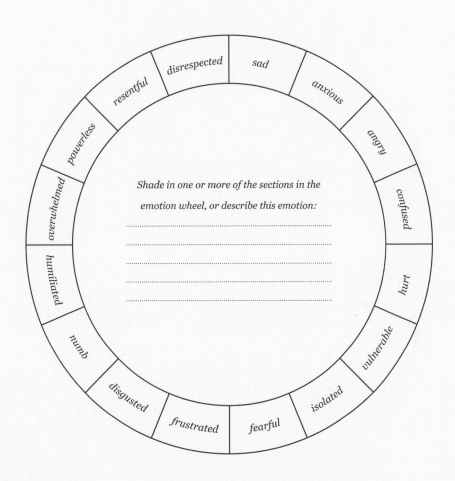

Shade in one or more of the sections in the emotion wheel, or describe this emotion:

Reflect on a time when you experienced racial apathy. How did this experience impact your ability to honor your pain?

....
....
....
....

Think about the type of care you needed at that time. What are some ways you would like to honor your pain moving forward?

....
....
....
....
....
....
....
....
....
....
....
....
....
....
....
....
....
....
....

If you find yourself experiencing racial apathy, try repeating these affirmations:

I won't let anyone rob me of my right to feel my feelings.

I deserve to feel seen, heard, and held when I am hurting.

My ability to hurt means that I am in touch with my humanity.

TENDER REMINDER

You are a whole person navigating a fragmented system. Honor your wholeness by allowing yourself the space to feel and express your hurt.

Recalling Your Goodness

EXPLORING RACIAL FEAR

Racial fear is the irrational fear or paranoia that Black, Indigenous, and people of color are dangerous. It often shows up as unpredictable reactions directed at communities of color, which can make us feel like we constantly need to take precautions around white people so that they do not harm us.

People develop racial fear by being conditioned to believe that BIPOC are "up to no good." In his work on racialized trauma, psychotherapist Resmaa Menakem discusses how white people often confuse their irrational fear with danger. In turn, they feel entitled to reacting in harmful ways. However, irrational fear is *never* a justification for being harmful. There is a difference between a real threat and a perceived threat rooted in bias. Someone *feeling threatened* by a person of color does not necessarily mean that they are actually *being threatened* by a person of color.

I recall rushing home one evening, and there was a white man a couple meters up the sidewalk from me. When he saw me walking in his general direction, his eyes filled with fear. He reeled his body away and glared at me; he was frightened by the idea of a Black person walking swiftly in his direction. I was deeply offended because I knew that person's fear about my Blackness was not based on reality—it was based on white imagination, which views Black people as a threat. In actuality, *whiteness endangers us*.

Incidents like this put us in a position where we need to "prove" that we are nonthreatening. There is something heartbreaking about having to police ourselves so that we aren't policed by others. My hope is that we learn not to blame ourselves for people's racial fear—and that we continue to believe in the love in our hearts.

RACIST FEAR

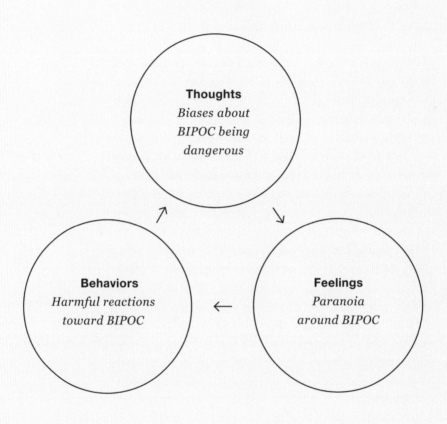

Thoughts
*Biases about
BIPOC being
dangerous*

Behaviors
*Harmful reactions
toward BIPOC*

Feelings
*Paranoia
around BIPOC*

HOW RACIAL FEAR MANIFESTS

While the widespread paranoia about Black, Indigenous, and people of color is rooted in unfounded biases, the ways in which it manifests are real. It can produce hateful reactions in the form of three widely recognized fear responses: fight, flight, and freeze. The "fight or flight" response was coined by physiologist Walter Bradford Cannon.

Here's what these responses look like with racial fear:

Fight | Fighting off the perceived threat

- *A store owner follows a Latine person around the grocery store.*
- *A white person clutches their bag as they walk past a Black person.*
- *Someone attacks an East Asian person due to racist thoughts associated with COVID-19.*
- *A white person calls the police when they see a Black person walking in their neighborhood.*
- *An airport security agent targets a South Asian Muslim passenger at a security checkpoint.*

Flight | Fleeing from the perceived threat

- *A passenger avoids sitting next to Black people on public transportation.*
- *A passerby crosses the street when they see a Black person on the same sidewalk as them.*
- *White families move out of neighborhoods that have Black residents.*
- *A coworker or peer avoids a Black person because they find them intimidating.*
- *A person avoids a group of Black people congregating in a space.*

Freeze | Remaining still until the perceived threat passes

- *A driver locks their car door when a Black person walks past them.*
- *A pedestrian notices a Latine man walking behind them and steps aside until they pass.*
- *A person waits for the next elevator when they see a Black person on it.*

THE IMPACT OF RACIAL FEAR

Here are some of the ways racial fear can impact you:

- It can cause you to become avoidant and reclusive.
- It can cause you to view yourself as a "troublemaker."
- It can cause you to experience *genuine* fear, anxiety, and hesitance around white people.
- It can cause you to constantly reassure others of your innocence by being overly polite and accommodating.
- It can cause you to alter your appearance, dress, speech, and behavior to help you come across as a good-natured person.

I often reflect on Brent Staples's essay "Just Walk on By," in which he shares, "I now take precautions to make myself less threatening. I move about with care, particularly late in the evening. I give a wide berth to nervous people on subway platforms during the wee hours, particularly when I have exchanged business clothes for jeans. If I happen to be entering a building behind some people who appear skittish, I may walk by, letting them clear the lobby before I return, so as not to seem to be following them. I have been calm and extremely congenial on those rare occasions when I've been pulled over by the police."

This need to constantly walk on eggshells to prove our innocence is an emotionally draining experience. This is why finding ways to remember the good in our hearts is critical to preserving ourselves.

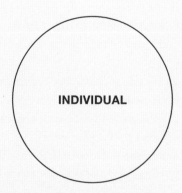

INDIVIDUAL

**HOW TO TEND
TO YOURSELF**

Affirm Your Goodness

Engage in rituals that remind you of who you truly are. You can do the following:

- Make time for play. Being consistently criminalized can rob us of our inherent playfulness.
- Repeat a personal mantra that speaks to your goodness, or create a list of the values and qualities that you are grateful to have.
- Connect with friends, family, or loved ones who can remind you of the goodness in your heart.

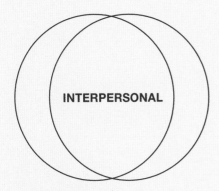

INTERPERSONAL

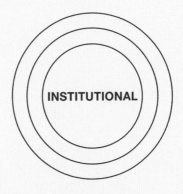

INSTITUTIONAL

Reject Stereotypes

When you witness people perpetuating stereotypes about BIPOC being dangerous, challenge them. You can do this by saying the following:

- "I don't agree with how this book/movie/article portrays BIPOC as dangerous."
- "I'm getting the sense that you feel unsafe around Black people, which is harmful because this fear is rooted in racist narratives."
- "What you just said insinuates that BIPOC are threatening."
- "I don't find it funny when people make jokes that criminalize my community."
- "Using terms such as thug/terrorist/illegal to refer to communities of color is highly racist."

Support Decriminalization

The systemic criminalization of BIPOC is a prominent example of how racial fear manifests. You can advocate for decriminalization by doing the following:

- Support organizations that work to abolish carceral systems that criminalize BIPOC through school-to-prison pipelines, racial profiling, and mass incarceration.
- Elevate initiatives and organizations that counter the negative stereotypes people have about BIPOC. These stereotypes are often what lead to deeply harmful fear-based reactions toward us.

Reflection

Take a moment to explore how racial fear makes you feel.

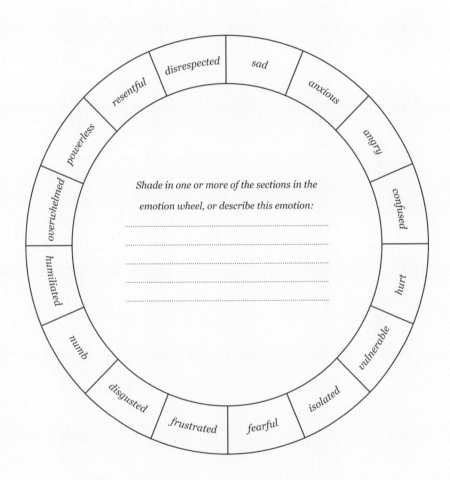

disrespected

sad

resentful

anxious

powerless

angry

overwhelmed

confused

humiliated

hurt

numb

vulnerable

disgusted

isolated

frustrated

fearful

Shade in one or more of the sections in the emotion wheel, or describe this emotion:

Reflect on a time when you were subjected to racial fear. In what ways did this experience make you feel like you had to prove your goodness?

....
....
....
....

Think about the stereotypes that contributed to this experience. What are some ways that you can reaffirm who you truly are despite them?

....
....
....
....
....
....
....
....
....
....
....
....
....
....
....
....
....

When you find yourself experiencing racial fear, try repeating these affirmations:

I believe in my inherent goodness.

I will not align with stories that vilify my community.

People's inability to see my humanity reflects what is in their hearts, not mine.

TENDER REMINDER

You deserve to live a life that doesn't ask you to police yourself for your goodness to be felt.

A Love Note

ON PLEASURE

The heaviness of our experiences with white supremacist culture can make us feel like we don't deserve to be playful, care-
free, and joyous. So much so that many of us believe that our
stories simply do not encompass pleasure. In the moments
when pleasure does arrive, we forget how to surrender to it. We
forget how to revel in our laughter, dance, song, food, community, creativity, and love—all of which are also part of the human
experience.

I want it to be known that our stories are not just about our suffering. This does not mean that we should bypass the heaviness
we hold in our hearts. These feelings are valid and are meant to
be felt. It simply means that we are whole, and being whole is a
practice of intimately knowing both our pain and our pleasure.

In the moments when pleasure knocks on our door, I hope more
of us will have the opportunity to invite it in, spend time with
it, and hold it close. I integrate pleasure into my life by indulg-
ing in belly laughs, cooking a tender meal, reveling in scents
that remind me of a time before, listening to music, sitting with
nature, reading books that my hands cannot put down, dancing under the sun, learning about the design of things, and
acknowledging when warm winds kiss my skin.

If you feel called to, take a moment to reflect on what holding
pleasure looks like, feels like, and sounds like to you.

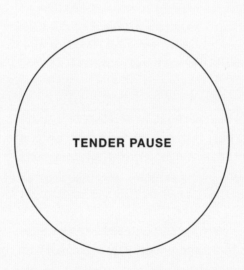

TENDER PAUSE

Take a break, breathe, and tend to your heart before moving on to the next section of this racial wellness journey.

You deserve to experience ease.

Mental Wellness

The following chapters explore how racism can impact our minds, and offer guidance on how we can alleviate some of this mental disharmony.

Validating
Your Reality

EXPLORING RACIAL GASLIGHTING

Gaslighting is a form of psychological abuse used to make another person question their thoughts, feelings, and reality. Although gaslighting is a tactic that more and more people are beginning to understand, particularly in unhealthy romantic, platonic, or familial relationships, racial gaslighting is a tactic that not many are able to recognize.

Racial gaslighting is when Black, Indigenous, and people of color confront the ways they have experienced racism, and an individual, group, or institution (such as the media, legal system, or government) tries to make them doubt their experience, often to maintain control, avoid taking accountability, or conduct normalized racial abuse. This concept was first developed by Professor Angelique M. Davis and Rose Ernst, who define racial gaslighting as a process that perpetuates and normalizes a white supremacist reality.

Those of us who experience racism know when it is taking place. We know what it *looks like*, *sounds like*, and *feels like*. From lifetimes of having our ancestors, community members, family, friends, and ourselves experience it, we can sense it deep in our bones. Still, I cannot count the number of times that I have been gaslit after expressing my truths. Every time it happens, I am left wondering how my lived experience became a matter of debate.

When we consider the harm that BIPOC experience at the hands of white supremacy, *it makes sense* that we have negative thoughts and feelings about it. Anger, sadness, and frustration are normal responses to being violated. And yet in so many ways, we have been taught that if we do not swallow the pain of our oppression, there is something wrong with us.

RACIAL GASLIGHTING

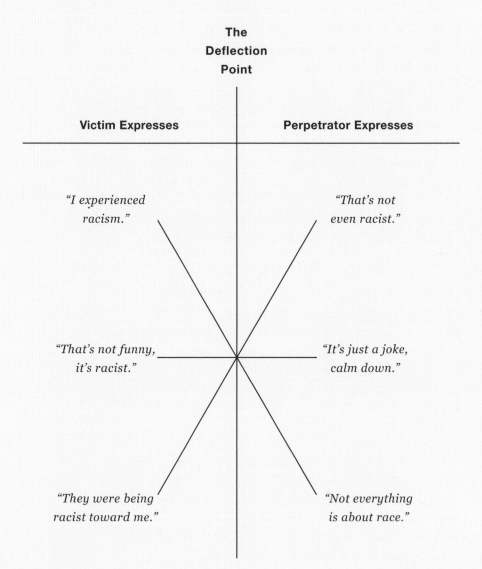

The Deflection Point

Victim Expresses

Perpetrator Expresses

"I experienced racism."

"That's not even racist."

"That's not funny, it's racist."

"It's just a joke, calm down."

"They were being racist toward me."

"Not everything is about race."

HOW RACIAL GASLIGHTING MANIFESTS

Racial gaslighting usually occurs when Black, Indigenous, and people of color confront a perpetrator such as a person, group, or institution about their racist behavior. After being confronted, perpetrators aim to undermine our thoughts, feelings, and experiences by using a strategy coined by Jennifer Freyd called DARVO: deny, attack, and reverse the roles of the victim and offender. Freyd first used this term in 1997 to address power dynamics in unhealthy relationships.

Here is what DARVO can look like when it comes to racism:

DENY

Dismissal	The perpetrator completely denies the harm they caused. *"What I said or did is not racist."*
Exceptionalism	The perpetrator tries to distinguish themselves from others. *"I'm not racist. I'm not like other white people."*
Questioning	The perpetrator tries to question your memory. *"It wasn't because of race. It's not always about that."*
Trivializing	The perpetrator tries to downplay the harm they caused. *"It was just a joke, calm down."*
Credentialing	The perpetrator begins to highlight the other BIPOC that they know. *"I'm not racist, I have Black friends."*

ATTACK

Threatening

The perpetrator tries to silence you by using intimidation tactics.

"I'm not going to talk to you if you make everything about race."

Tone policing

The perpetrator focuses on how you react instead of their action.

"If you said it calmly, maybe I would listen to you."

Debate-club racism

The perpetrator tries to argue instead of admitting harm.

"Just to play devil's advocate . . ."

Punishing

The perpetrator punishes you to teach you a lesson.

A Black, Indigenous, or person of color loses their job for speaking out against racism in the workplace.

Discrediting

The perpetrator tries to tarnish your reputation to prevent others from believing your truth.

The media portrays Black victims of police brutality as people with questionable backgrounds.

REVERSE VICTIM AND OFFENDER

Projection	The perpetrator begins to attribute their own behaviors to you. *"I'm not racist, you're racist" or "You bringing up racism is why racism still exists!"*
Intent over impact	The perpetrator centers their intentions over the impact they had on you. *"I didn't mean it like that—I'm a good person."*
"White tears"	The perpetrator weaponizes their emotions. *Crying after being called a racist so that they can be viewed as the victim.*
Oppression Olympics	The perpetrator centers on their own experiences. *"I'm not racist—I'm oppressed, too!"*
Victim blaming	The perpetrator tries to make it seem like you deserved the harm you experienced. *Blaming Black people for the harm they experience at the hands of racist police.*

THE IMPACT OF RACIAL GASLIGHTING

Here are some of the ways racial gaslighting can impact you:

- It can cause you to silence yourself.
- It can cause anxiety and depression.
- It can make you think that you're the problem.
- It can cause you to minimize your feelings.
- It can make you question your experiences with racism.

Racial gaslighting can make it difficult for us to trust our responses to our reality. In turn, our *natural reactions* to oppression, such as anger and sadness, are repressed. In the moments when we should speak out, we become silent, unsure, and afraid. This is the purpose of gaslighting—to make us accomplices in protecting the abuse we experience. This is why it is incredibly important that we find ways to identify, understand, and challenge racial gaslighting so that we may speak truth to power.

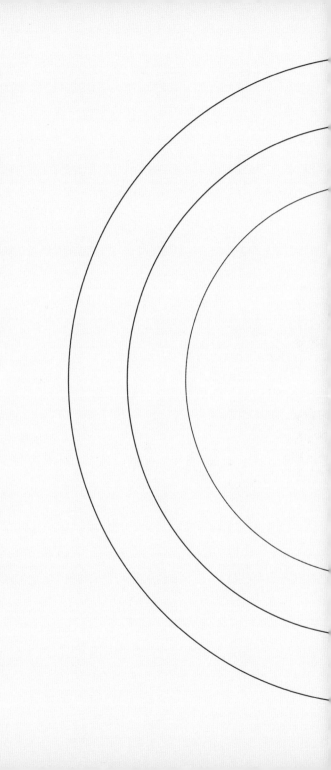

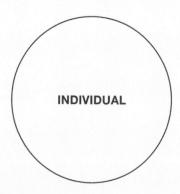

INDIVIDUAL

**HOW TO TEND
TO YOURSELF**

Validate Yourself

One of the most important things you can get as someone experiencing racial gaslighting is validation. You can validate your thoughts, feelings, and experiences by doing the following:

- Share your experiences with people who understand what it feels like to experience racism.
- Take the time to document your experiences by journaling, recording comments, and taking videos or photos of harmful incidents.
- Engage with anti-oppressive teachers, activists, or therapists who can help you identify, unpack, and validate your experiences with racial oppression.

Racial Wellness

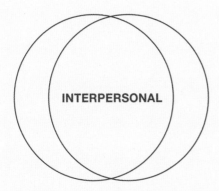

INTERPERSONAL

INSTITUTIONAL

Stand Firm in What You Know

Do not exhaust yourself arguing with someone who is more concerned about being called racist than they are with their actions. Instead, set boundaries by saying the following:

- "I will not engage in a debate to prove my lived experiences to you."
- "I am fully aware of, clearly remember, and deeply comprehend what happened."
- "It is clear that you can't identify with my experience, but that doesn't make it any less real."
- "Your memories may not align with mine, but I will honor my truth anyway."

Amplify the Truth

Find ways to disrupt the narratives that our experiences with racism aren't real by doing the following:

- Participate in protests. Protests can serve as a space for you to express your thoughts, truths, and feelings about racist institutions.
- Support racial justice organizations that amplify the prevalence of racism perpetuated by institutions. Supporting the work of liberatory truth tellers is critical to ensuring that our reality is accurately depicted.

Reflection

Take a moment to explore how racial gaslighting makes you feel.

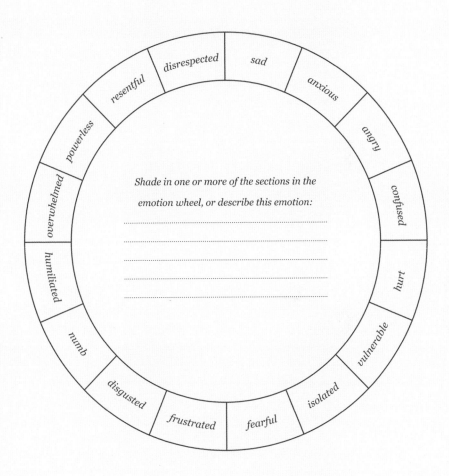

disrespected

sad

resentful

anxious

powerless

angry

overwhelmed

confused

Shade in one or more of the sections in the
emotion wheel, or describe this emotion:

....

....

....

....

....

humiliated

hurt

numb

vulnerable

disgusted

isolated

frustrated

fearful

Reflect on a time when you were racially gaslit. In what ways did it cause you to minimize or question your lived experience?

....

....

....

....

Think about the validation you needed at the time. What are some ways you would like to validate your truths moving forward?

....

....

....

....

....

....

....

....

....

....

....

....

....

....

....

....

....

....

....

REMEMBER
Your thoughts, feelings, and reactions to racism mean the
following is happening:

*Your body is triggered
by this system.*

*You do not deserve this
treatment.*

*Your boundaries have
been violated.*

TENDER REMINDER

Your resistance
to your oppression
tells you that you
love yourself.
Don't let anybody
talk you out of loving
yourself.

Uncovering the Truth

EXPLORING RACIAL TRIANGULATION

Triangulation is a manipulation tactic that involves three people: a perpetrator and two victims. The perpetrator pulls one victim into a conflict and manipulates them into joining forces against the other victim. The perpetrator incites chaos to deflect from the harm they've caused and to maintain control.

Racial triangulation speaks to the ways white supremacist culture has weaponized Black, Indigenous, and people of color against one another. The goal of racial triangulation is to create division between communities of color experiencing racial abuse so that we are unable to work together and dismantle white supremacy. The term *racial triangulation* was coined by Professor Claire J. Kim, whose work highlights the ways in which white supremacist culture triangulates Asian people. While Kim has since expressed that because she did not fully understand the nature of anti-Blackness at the time, she no longer agrees with the ways she framed racial triangulation—the concept of divide and conquer still rings true.

Racial triangulation as a divide-and-conquer tactic often involves blaming one community of color for another's problems, bribing one with resources in exchange for their participation in oppressing another, and creating narratives that cultivate mistrust between them. By *manufacturing conflict*, white supremacist culture puts BIPOC in positions where we begin to behave in oppressive ways toward one another. As we become enveloped in our own conflict, we lose sight of the fact that white supremacist culture is oppressing *all of us*. To get free, we must become co-conspirators in the struggle. The power to overpower white supremacy lies in community.

RACIAL TRIANGULATION

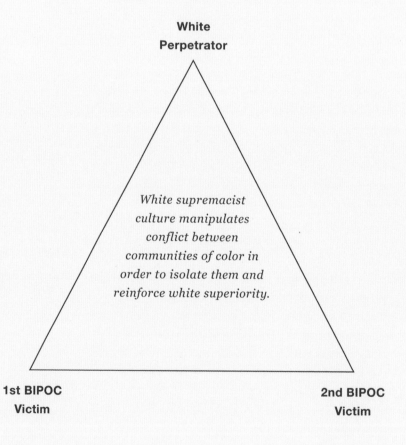

White
Perpetrator

*White supremacist
culture manipulates
conflict between
communities of color in
order to isolate them and
reinforce white superiority.*

1st BIPOC
Victim

2nd BIPOC
Victim

HOW RACIAL TRIANGULATION MANIFESTS

Racial triangulation works by perpetuating narratives that create division between Black, Indigenous, and people of color on intercommunity and intracommunity levels to deflect from the ways in which white supremacist culture harms all of us and maintains white superiority.

Here is what racial triangulation can look like:

Racial Hierarchy	White supremacist culture creates a hierarchy of race that ranks white people at the top, non-Black communities of color in the middle, and Black people at the bottom.

1.) **DIVIDE:** Non-Black communities of color begin to internalize anti-Blackness and try to distance themselves from being associated with Blackness by mistreating and discriminating against Black people.

2.) **DEFLECT:** Attention is diverted from the white supremacist culture's role in creating a hierarchy in which one's proximity to whiteness determines how they are treated in society.

3.) **CONTROL:** White supremacist culture gets to justify the mistreatment of *all* BIPOC because everyone has, either knowingly or unknowingly, bought into the idea that whiteness is superior.

The Model Minority Myth

White supremacist culture creates the narrative that East Asians are more hardworking, successful, and intelligent than Black, Indigenous, Latine, and other people of color.

1. **DIVIDE:** Asian people and other non-Black communities of color begin to view Black and Latine people as lazy and blame them for any barriers to achievement they may experience.

2. **DEFLECT:** Attention is diverted from the ways in which white supremacist culture builds structures, policies, and practices that create barriers to upward mobility for all communities of color.

3. **CONTROL:** White supremacist culture gets to justify divesting from equitable policies that could improve the upward mobility of *all* BIPOC, such as affirmative action.

Resource Hoarding

White supremacist culture creates the narrative that documented immigrants are deserving of opportunities and resources, but undocumented BIPOC immigrants are taking them away.

1. **DIVIDE:** Documented BIPOC immigrants begin to view undocumented BIPOC immigrants as a threat to the limited opportunities and resources they have.

2. **DEFLECT:** Attention is diverted from the ways in which white supremacist culture hoards opportunities and resources for white people by making it harder for BIPOC to access them.

3. **CONTROL:** White supremacist culture gets to justify its inhumane exclusion, treatment, and exploitation of undocumented immigrants.

Anti-Asian Violence | White supremacist culture created the narrative that Black people were disproportionately violent toward East Asian communities at the height of COVID-19.

1. **DIVIDE:** East Asian communities and society at large begin to feed into narratives that Black people are dangerous.

2. **DEFLECT:** Attention is diverted from the fact that studies have shown that most anti-Asian hate crimes in the United States are committed by white people (one study reported that 75 percent of anti-Asian hate perpetrators were white men).

3. **CONTROL:** White supremacist culture gets to justify its continued profiling, policing, and incarceration of Black communities.

Colorism | White supremacist culture creates the narrative that BIPOC with lighter skin tones are more worthy than BIPOC with darker skin tones.

1. **DIVIDE:** BIPOC begin to internalize colorism and mistreat people with dark skin within their own communities.

2. **DEFLECT:** Attention is diverted from white supremacist culture's role in creating a hierarchy where one's proximity to whiteness (in this case their skin tone) determines their treatment in society.

3. **CONTROL:** White supremacist culture gets to justify its preferential treatment of people with lighter skin because everyone has bought into the idea that whiteness (or lightness) is superior.

THE IMPACT OF RACIAL TRIANGULATION

Here are some of the ways that racial triangulation can impact you:

- It can cause you to internalize anti-Blackness.
- It can cause you to harbor resentment toward other BIPOC.
- It can cause you to compete with other BIPOC.
- It can cause you to value whiteness and devalue anything that doesn't adhere to it.
- It can cause you to believe and perpetuate racist stereotypes about other BIPOC, including those in your own community.

Racial triangulation has a sinister way of making Black, Indigenous, and people of color collude with the white supremacist agenda. When I reflect on this, my mind always goes back to writer Audre Lorde's words: "The master's tools will never dismantle the master's house." These words remind us that we cannot dismantle racial oppression by using the same tools of the oppressor on one another. We must create *new* tools, and we must do it *together* if we want to be effective in liberating the collective.

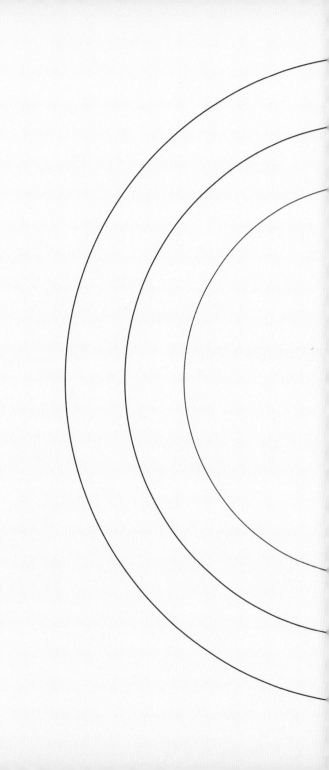

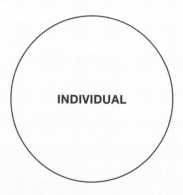

INDIVIDUAL

**HOW TO TEND
TO YOURSELF**

Increase Your Awareness

What makes racial triangulation so successful is the fact that it thrives from BIPOC not knowing how whiteness functions. You can protect yourself by doing the following:

- Study the history, goals, and strategies behind white supremacist culture.
- Learn how to identify the signs of triangulation (both racial and nonracial).
- Take the time to understand how various communities of color are differently or similarly affected by white supremacy.

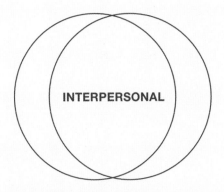

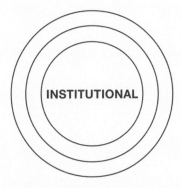

Reflect Before You React

When people intentionally create false narratives to divide people of color, it is helpful to take the following steps:

1. Express that it is a false narrative or a narrative that has been taken out of context.
2. Make it clear that you do not agree with the narrative they are sharing, and explain why, if you have the capacity.
3. Set boundaries with the person by removing yourself from the conversation.
4. Take the space to process the ways in which white supremacy works to divide and conquer BIPOC by connecting with friends, allies, or activists who understand.

Support Community Building

When racial triangulation is perpetuated by institutions, it is important that we strengthen our community-building efforts. This is what it can look like:

- Join BIPOC coalitions that center our shared struggle against white supremacy and encourage us to invest in one another's liberation from racist institutions.

- Organize healing spaces, such as online forums or support groups where BIPOC can process the ways in which white supremacy works to divide and conquer us, and work to repair any intracommunity and intercommunity harm that has taken place in the past or present.

Reflection

Take a moment to explore how racial triangulation makes you feel.

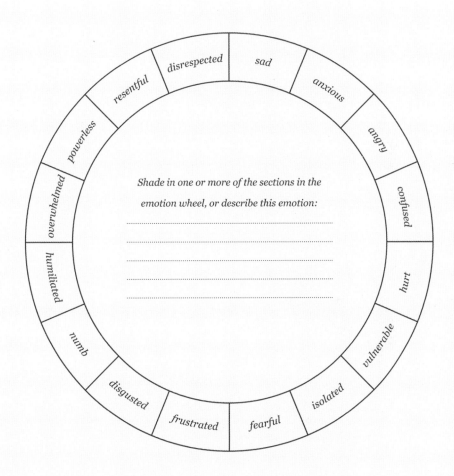

resentful
disrespected
sad
anxious
angry
powerless
confused
overwhelmed
humiliated
hurt
numb
vulnerable
disgusted
isolated
frustrated
fearful

Shade in one or more of the sections in the
emotion wheel, or describe this emotion:

Reflect on some of the narratives you have heard being used to divide BIPOC. How have these narratives impacted your relationship with other people of color?

....
....
....
....

Racial triangulation is often used to disrupt BIPOC liberatory movements. What could you do to help preserve our movements?

....
....
....
....
....
....
....
....
....
....
....
....
....
....
....
....
....
....
....

When you find yourself experiencing racial triangulation, repeat these affirmations:

I choose community over hierarchy.

I will unite and build in the face of divide and conquer.

I can practice self-care while also practicing community care.

TENDER REMINDER

Your humanity
weaves into the
humanity of other
Black, Indigenous,
and people of color.
When we liberate
each other, we
liberate ourselves.

A Love Note

ON INTUITION

White supremacist culture functions to leave us in a state of shock, confusion, and disarray. This is common in psychologically abusive dynamics. When you try to address harmful behavior in an abusive dynamic, you suddenly find yourself in the midst of psychological warfare. It is all a distraction to make us lose sight of our needs, our truths, and what it is that we are fighting for.

When we are being manipulated in this way, we are less likely to recognize how deeply violent the system is. What can help keep us grounded is our intuition—our ability to instinctively know something without analytical reasoning. Connecting to our intuition gives us clarity around the fact that nothing about white supremacist culture is normal or okay. It helps us stand up against oppressive systems and say, "This doesn't *feel right* and it is in my *best interest* to resist."

I want more of us to be able to stay close to our inherent knowing. I lean into my intuition by honoring the initial feeling I get about something, someplace, or someone; processing harmful incidents with people I trust; asking myself what I actually want and need; being observant; checking in with myself; journaling about my experiences and my truths; making space for silent reflection; being honest about how something hurt me; setting boundaries; and honoring my righteous rage.

If you feel called to, take a moment to reflect on what connecting to your intuition looks, feels, and sounds like to you.

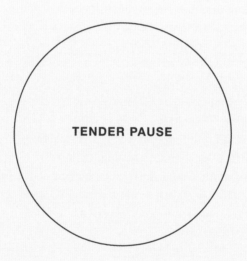

TENDER PAUSE

Take a break, breathe, and tend to _your mind_ before moving on to the next section of this racial wellness journey.

Physical Wellness

You deserve to revel in bodily freedom.

The following chapters explore how racism impacts our bodies, and offer guidance on how we can expel some of this embodied heaviness.

Soothing Your System

EXPLORING RACIAL VIOLENCE

Racial violence in the form of harassment and assault is a type of abuse intended to threaten, injure, or end the lives of Black, Indigenous, and people of color. It is fueled by a deep sense of lovelessness. White supremacist culture not only dehumanizes us but also demonizes us. These two processes combine to make it easier for people to perpetuate or justify harm against us.

Racial violence can be committed by individuals, groups, or institutions, and it often takes place in everyday life. Whether we are jogging, driving, sleeping, playing, attending class, going to a place of worship, or grocery shopping, it is not uncommon to hear about a Black, Indigenous, or person of color going about their day and becoming a victim of a racist attack.

When we experience or witness racial violence, it can activate our nervous system, our body's control center. Messages sent from our brain control our thoughts, movements, and responses. Racial violence creates an *embodied alertness*, otherwise known as *hypervigilance*. Hypervigilance causes us to constantly anticipate or scan for danger in our surrounding environment. When we are hypervigilant, we may keep an eye out for behaviors that seem threatening, avoid certain places that pose a threat, and even warn other Black, Indigenous, and people of color about potential threats.

After widely publicized racially violent incidents happen, I often go through periods of feeling nervous to take a walk, to go jogging, to wear a hoodie—to do any of the things that the people who were my skin color did before they were harmed. While some may pathologize this behavior as paranoia, this is not the case. Systemic racial violence creates this *valid* feeling of unsafety within our bodies. It makes sense for us to try to look out for ourselves. Our visceral responses to living in a racially unsafe world are an act of self-preservation.

RACIAL VIOLENCE

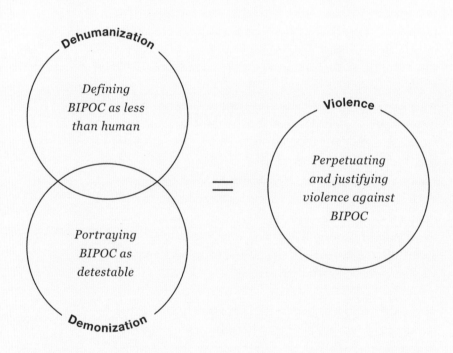

Dehumanization

Defining
BIPOC as less
than human

Portraying
BIPOC as
detestable

Demonization

Violence

Perpetuating
and justifying
violence against
BIPOC

HOW RACIAL VIOLENCE MANIFESTS

Racial violence typically shows up as verbal, physical, or property violence, as well as acts of terror toward Black, Indigenous, and people of color.

Here's what racial violence can look like:

VERBAL VIOLENCE
- *Yelling out racial slurs at BIPOC*
- *Threatening to injure or end someone's life because of their race*
- *Using racist language to incite violence against BIPOC*

PHYSICAL VIOLENCE
- *Police brutality against BIPOC*
- *Racial profiling and "stop-and-frisk" practices*
- *Physically assaulting someone due to their race*

PROPERTY VIOLENCE
- *Vandalizing a space with racist graffiti*
- *Destroying someone's personal property because of their race*
- *Displaying racist memorabilia and flags on homes, cars, storefronts, and other places*

ACTS OF TERROR
- *Racially motivated and planned attacks such as arson, bombings, and shootings in neighborhoods, schools, community centers, or religious spaces*

THE IMPACT OF RACIAL VIOLENCE

Here are some of the ways racial violence can impact you:

- It can lead to anxiety and chronic stress.
- It can lead to elevated blood pressure.
- It can make it difficult for you to sleep.
- It can make you easily startled and on edge.
- It can cause you to ruminate about being harmed.
- It can give you tense muscles, clenched fists, and a clenched jaw.

Our brains are wired to be aware of the dangers in our surroundings. Being able to sense danger is what keeps us safe. However, racial violence activates our fear responses for prolonged periods of time. We shouldn't have to be hyperaware or have our guard up all the time. Feeling like we cannot be safe on the street, in our cars, in our homes, or in our beds can significantly impact our nervous system. This is why it is so important that we find ways to soothe ourselves when we can.

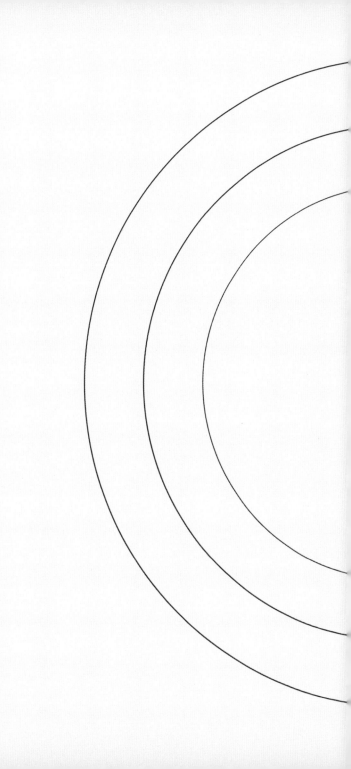

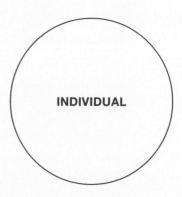

INDIVIDUAL

**HOW TO TEND
TO YOURSELF**

Practice Self-Soothing

Hypervigilance is a valid response to a chronic threat. Practice calming your nervous system by doing the following:

- Create a grounding ritual. Spend time in nature, experiment with sound healing practices such as humming, take calming herbal supplements, and engage in self-touch practices such as hugging yourself or tapping, which involves lightly tapping acupressure points on your body.
- Spend time with people who make you feel safe. In a society that causes us to be on high alert, it is important that we connect with people who allow us to breathe a little easier.
- Speak to a trauma-informed therapist who understands the impact of racial violence and can give you guidance on how to process your experiences.

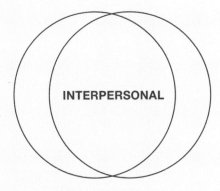

Create a Safety Plan

No one should have to create a safety plan because of their identity. However, as we continue the fight to dismantle white supremacist culture, having one can be helpful. This can involve the following:

- Create a habitual safety check-in with people you know you can depend on.
- Surround yourself with people who know how to identify racial hostility and violence so that you feel less alone.
- Set up community care efforts such as walking or driving each other home and warning each other about areas that are unsafe for BIPOC.
- Build community defense initiatives that protect us from verbal, physical, and other forms of racial hostility and violence.

Challenge Systemic Violence

To challenge racial violence on institutional levels, we must develop both proactive and reactive ways of protecting BIPOC lives. Here is how you can do this:

- Advocate for widespread anti-racist and anti-colonial education. These forms of education prevent violence by encouraging people to reject racially harmful thoughts, feelings, and behavior.
- Support abolitionist organizations that explore ways to protect us from racial violence. We need trustworthy systems that deter people from committing harm and ensure that people who do are held accountable for their behavior.

Reflection

Take a moment to explore how racial violence makes you feel.

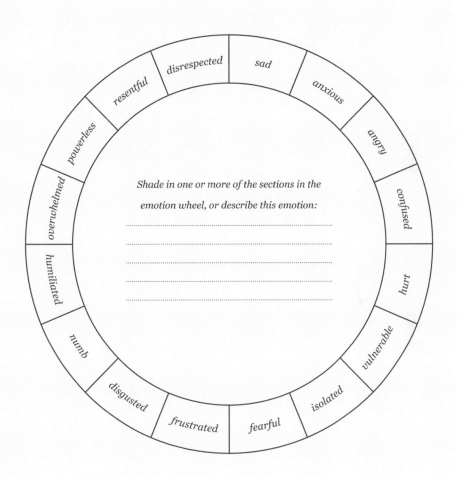

resentful · disrespected · sad · anxious · angry · powerless · overwhelmed · confused · humiliated · hurt · numb · vulnerable · disgusted · isolated · frustrated · fearful

Shade in one or more of the sections in the emotion wheel, or describe this emotion:

Reflect on how racial violence has impacted the way you show up in the world. How does hypervigilance live in your body?

....
....
....
....

Envision what bodily safety looks and feels like to you. What are some ways we can collectively actualize this vision?

....
....
....
....
....
....
....
....
....
....
....
....
....
....
....
....
....
....
....

When you find yourself navigating racial violence,
repeat these affirmations:

I deserve to be protected.

*I deserve to experience
the freedom of safety.*

*I believe that we can and
will build communal
systems that protect us.*

TENDER REMINDER

You deserved to feel protected the moment you were born. Being robbed of your sense of safety is not your legacy.

Tending to Your Body

EXPLORING RACIAL INEQUITY

Racial inequity speaks to the unfair distribution of resources and opportunities between white people and Black, Indigenous, and people of color. It is caused by racist structures, policies, and practices that ensure that BIPOC experience disadvantages when it comes to education, employment, healthcare, housing, and more. Often referred to as the *social determinants of health*, these factors can affect our physical well-being.

When we experience a threat, our body's stress response is activated. After the threat is gone, our stress response deactivates. However, because racism is systemic, the threat is ever-present. As the adversity we experience accumulates, it triggers a prolonged response within us called *toxic stress*, causing a long-term impact on our physical bodies.

This process is known as *racial weathering*. The weathering hypothesis was formed by public health professor Arline Geronimus, who found that the physical health of Black women can deteriorate in early adulthood due to cumulative racism and its socioeconomic impact. Also known as *John Henryism*, a term coined by public health researcher Sherman A. James, there is a fundamental connection between racism, stress, and their collective impact on the body.

Racial weathering can lead to issues such as high blood pressure, chronic illness, and a shorter life expectancy. It is why we often see deep health disparities between racial groups—they stem from the racist environment we live in, not individual habits. Because we experience barriers to ease, racism causes us to *embody* dis-ease.

RACIAL INEQUITY

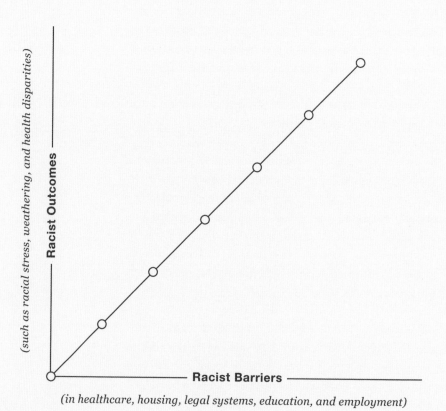

HOW RACIAL INEQUITY MANIFESTS

Racial inequity shows up in all areas of our lives. It is created by structural barriers to education, employment, healthcare, housing, and community.

Here's what racial inequity can look like:

EDUCATION

- *Cities fail to allocate resources to predominantly BIPOC schools.*
- *Teachers give Black and Latine students lower scores and grades based on racial biases.*
- *Admissions committees deny BIPOC acceptance to schools, colleges, and universities.*

EMPLOYMENT

- *Employers refuse to hire Black and Latine talent.*
- *Employers pay Black and Latine employees less than their white colleagues.*
- *Employers refuse to promote BIPOC to executive, decision-making positions.*

HEALTHCARE

- *Healthcare workers neglect the needs, concerns, and emergencies of BIPOC patients.*
- *Doctors fail to understand how certain illnesses may present on darker skin tones.*
- *Cities fail to create affordable healthcare services in predominantly BIPOC neighborhoods.*

HOUSING

- *Banks deny BIPOC from getting mortgages, which prevents families from building generational wealth (i.e., redlining).*
- *Lenders charge BIPOC higher interest rates on mortgage loans, which often puts families into debt.*
- *Landlords increase rent prices in Black and brown neighborhoods*

(i.e., gentrification), which often pushes these communities of color out of their homes.

COMMUNITY

- *The mass incarceration of Black people leads to family separations and ruptures.*
- *Government agencies refuse to invest resources in predominantly BIPOC neighborhoods.*
- *Cities locate coal plants, chemical plants, and hazardous waste disposal near communities of color.*

THE IMPACT OF RACIAL INEQUITY

Here are some of the ways racial inequity can impact you:

- It can speed up your biological aging.
- It can lead to high cholesterol and hypertension.
- It can cause chronic inflammation and illness.
- It can cause you to work "twice as hard" in order to succeed.
- It can make you feel like adversity you face is due to your own shortcomings.

Black, Indigenous, and people of color experience racism from the minute we're born. Over the course of our lifetime, we deal with racism when we are learning, working, playing, living, and simply being. As we cope with the stress of having to navigate a racist society, our bodies may become mirrors of our lived experiences. My wish for us is that while we work to dismantle the structures that erode us, we find ways to tend to our bodies.

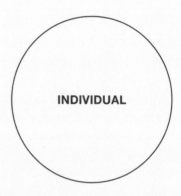

INDIVIDUAL

HOW TO TEND
TO YOURSELF

Honor Your Body

When our bodies are in a state of stress, it is important that we find small ways to decompress. Here is how you can do this:

- Replenish your body with different forms of deep rest.
- Engage in body movement therapies such as stretching, massage, breath work, dancing, acupuncture, and yoga.
- Work with a somatic therapist who can help release some of the tension trapped in your body.

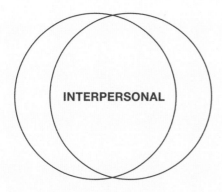

Center Collective Care

We can ease some of the toxic stress we experience because of racial inequity by providing or requesting help from mutual aid networks. Mutual aid networks perform these activities:

- Distribute food to ensure that individuals and families are nourished.
- Organize free health drives, clinics, and healing services.
- Send financial assistance to people struggling to make ends meet.
- Connect people in our communities to jobs and educational opportunities.
- Donate to community bail funds to help people who have been incarcerated.
- Join cooperatives that own, manage, and construct fair housing.

Confront Inequitable Practices

We can challenge racial inequity on an institutional level by demanding equitable practices, policies, and initiatives. Here is what this can look like:

- Amplify the work of public policy organizations that raise awareness about the *root causes behind* institutional racial inequity. This will help dispel myths that racial disparities are due to individual failures and make people more inclined to support equitable policies.
- Demand reparations by putting pressure on governments to enforce policies such as affirmative action, give land back to Indigenous peoples, compensate Black people impacted by slavery, and make amends to countries exploited by European colonization.

Reflection

Take a moment to explore how racial inequity makes you feel.

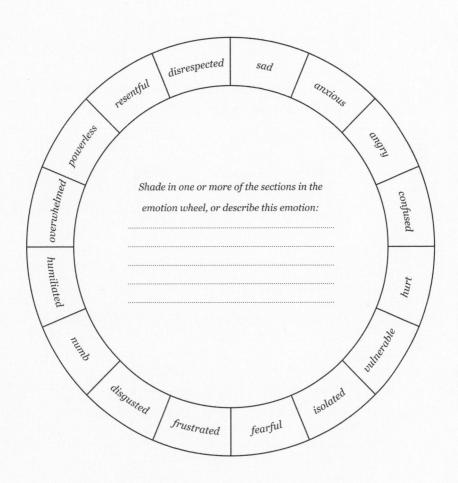

Shade in one or more of the sections in the emotion wheel, or describe this emotion:

disrespected, sad, anxious, angry, confused, hurt, vulnerable, isolated, fearful, frustrated, disgusted, numb, humiliated, overwhelmed, powerless, resentful

Reflect on your experiences with racial inequity. How have these experiences prevented you from having ease in your life?

....

....

....

....

....

What forms of support do you need in order to lessen the burden of racial inequity?

....

....

....

....

....

....

....

....

....

....

....

....

....

....

....

....

....

....

....

It can be helpful to repeat these affirmations when experiencing racial inequity:

I deserve to embody ease, not dis-ease.

Breathing, resting, and living are my birthright.

I honor my livelihood when I fight for racial equity.

TENDER REMINDER

Your story was never meant to be about surviving. You deserve to feel the ease that comes with thriving.

A Love Note

ON REST

We are taught that if we experience an injury, such as a twisted ankle, a sprained wrist, or a deep cut, our bodies need rest to recover. And yet, we don't always apply this same wisdom when it comes to navigating white supremacist culture.

In truth, when we experience racism on a daily basis, we come home with visible and invisible injuries. Our bodies need time and space to process this trauma through rest. Slowing down allows our bodies to regenerate by helping us conserve energy, build immunity, restore our cells, and fight inflammation. While rest alone cannot heal the chronic injury of experiencing racism, having a rest practice disrupts white supremacist and capitalist systems that thrive on our trauma.

When we rest, we transform our bodies from sites of domination to sites of liberation. It is these moments of ease that help alleviate the burden of existing in a system of dis-ease. I make room for rest by honoring my sleep schedule, holding on to silence when it visits me, lying down in nature, breathing in essential oils, letting myself daydream, drinking body-warming tea, escaping into a fiction novel, napping when my body asks for breaks, laying my head on a friend's shoulder, and listening to soothing music.

If you feel called to, take a moment to reflect on what prioritizing rest looks, feels, and sounds like to you.

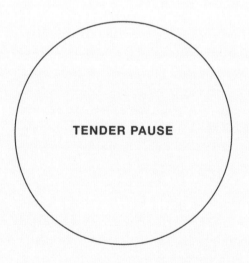

TENDER PAUSE

Take a break, breathe, and tend to y<u>our body</u> before moving on to the next section of this racial wellness journey.

Spiritual Wellness

You deserve to release loveless narratives.

The following chapters explore
the ways racism impacts
our sense of self, and provide
guidance on how we can resist
harmful internalizations.

Affirming
Your Dignity

EXPLORING RACIAL MICROAGGRESSIONS

Racial microaggressions are derogatory messages that Black, Indigenous, and people of color continuously receive about our racial identities. They can manifest as verbal and nonverbal abuse, and they come in the form of insults, criticism, eye-rolling, ignoring, and other forms of hostility. They reflect all the ways in which people have been conditioned to negatively view Black, Indigenous, and people of color.

The term *racial microaggressions* was coined by psychiatrist Chester D. Pierce. Due to the co-optation of the term *microaggressions* by white supremacist culture, there is a common misconception that it refers to experiences that are insignificant or have minimal impact because they often occur briefly. However, they are called microaggressions because they highlight forms of racism that are often *minimized* by white supremacist culture.

There is nothing micro about this form of harm. This mistreatment can condition us to feel like we are inferior, unintelligent, dangerous, lazy, unworthy, and don't belong. And yet, because of their habitualness and brevity, we may find ourselves questioning if what we are experiencing is important enough to confront.

I often refer to racial microaggressions as *racial dignity assaults* because I want to acknowledge that, due to the misinterpretation of the term, the word *micro* may cause perpetrators to feel like this form of harm is insignificant, and may cause Black, Indigenous, and people of color to feel invalidated. The term *racial dignity assault* helps us highlight how deeply these experiences can impact our sense of dignity. Psychologists who have researched microaggressions have called them "a death by a thousand cuts" because of the way they can create deep wounds.

RACIAL MICROAGGRESSIONS

Perceived message + impact

Actual message + impact

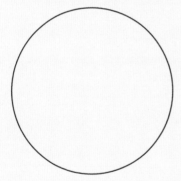
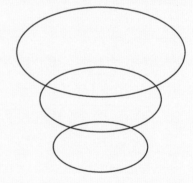

HOW RACIAL MICROAGGRESSIONS MANIFEST

Racial microaggressions *breathe* in our daily interactions. They can be subtle and unintentional, but they can also be explicit and intentional. They manifest verbally or nonverbally and *convey a deeper message* that degrades or invalidates Black, Indigenous, and people of color.

Here's what racial microaggressions look like:

VERBAL RACIAL MICROAGGRESSIONS

Action	Message
Someone uses racial slurs or tells a racist "joke."	*The perpetrator doesn't respect BIPOC.*
Someone says, "You got the job only because you're a diversity hire," or "You got into this school only because of affirmative action."	*The perpetrator is assuming that BIPOC are not as qualified as white people.*
Someone says, "You are so articulate," or "You're not like other [insert victim's race] people."	*The perpetrator finds it unusual for BIPOC to be intelligent or well-spoken.*
Someone says, "You're pretty for a [insert victim's race] person."	*The perpetrator doesn't find BIPOC attractive.*

NONVERBAL RACIAL MICROAGGRESSIONS

Action	Message
A patient who refuses to be treated by Black or brown doctors or nurses.	*The perpetrator finds it insulting to be served by someone they believe is inferior.*
A manager fails to reward the hard work of a BIPOC in the workplace.	*The perpetrator thinks BIPOC should work harder to achieve success in their careers.*
A teacher ignores BIPOC students in the classroom and caters only to white students.	*The perpetrator doesn't want to support or invest in the success of BIPOC.*
A taxi driver refuses to pick up BIPOC.	*The perpetrator doesn't want to be in close proximity to BIPOC.*

THE IMPACT OF RACIAL MICROAGGRESSIONS

Here are some of the ways racial microaggressions can impact you:

- They can increase stress, anxiety, and depression.
- They can cause you to feel confused, shocked, and invalidated.
- They can lead to low self-esteem, shame, and internalized inferiority.
- They can cause you to have intrusive repetitive thoughts about the incidents.
- They can cause you to feel guilt or hopelessness for not knowing how to respond or not responding the way you wish you had.

Racial microaggressions are a constant reminder to Black, Indigenous, and people of color that society perceives us as inferior to white people. Having to experience them almost every day of our lives can deplete our spirit. *Racial battle fatigue* is a term coined by psychologist William A. Smith to speak to the ways in which constantly experiencing dismissive, demeaning, insensitive, and hostile responses and environments can lead to exhaustion, frustration, and even a loss of our sense of self. To protect our dignity, we must find ways to affirm ourselves.

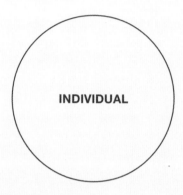

INDIVIDUAL

**HOW TO TEND
TO YOURSELF**

Give Yourself Grace

A common response to experiencing a racial microaggression is to feel guilt, disappointment, and shame. But remember, this burden is not ours to hold as the victims of harm. Give yourself grace by doing the following:

- Repeat affirmations about your identity to yourself to counter the narratives that you are not enough.
- Seek support from community. It is relieving to process racial microaggressions with people who understand what you're experiencing.
- Speak with a therapist who specializes in affirming BIPOC identities and can help you process the derogatory messages you receive.

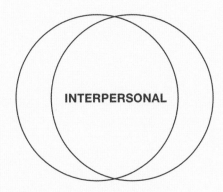

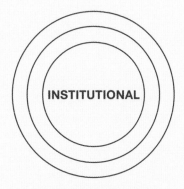

Create a Response Plan

Before you respond to a racial microaggression, it can be helpful to take a deep breath to collect yourself and decide if it is safe to address it and if you have the capacity to confront the perpetrator.

If you choose to address it, determine if it makes sense to do so verbally or nonverbally. While it is often said that nonverbal communication is passive, choosing not to verbally engage with someone after a racist experience can be an act of safety and self-preservation.

For more guidance on creating a response plan, see page 132.

Encourage Dignified Behavior

Put pressure on institutions to take action against racial microaggressions and uplift dignified ways of relating to one another. Here is how you can do this:

- Demand that your school or place of work invest in effective training on how to identify and disarm racial microaggressions to help transform environments into safe spaces for BIPOC.
- Use storytelling to condemn racial microaggressions enacted by and tolerated within institutions. In 2014, Black students at Harvard created the "I, Too, Am Harvard" photo campaign, which played an influential role in raising awareness about how *not to treat* BIPOC.

IF YOU DECIDE TO ADDRESS IT

VERBALLY

1

Ask the person to clarify what they did/said by saying, "What do you mean?" or "Why did you do/say that?" This forces the perpetrator to explain and directly address their problematic behavior.

2

Tell the person that what they did/said was not acceptable by saying, "That is problematic/That is harmful/I disagree."

3

Explain to them why their behavior was harmful to you and your community.

4

Seek support from others to help reduce the psychological impact.

NON-VERBALLY

1

Indicate that you disapprove of what they did/said by shaking your head, raising your eyebrows, frowning, or physically moving away.

2

Seek support from others to help reduce the psychological impact.

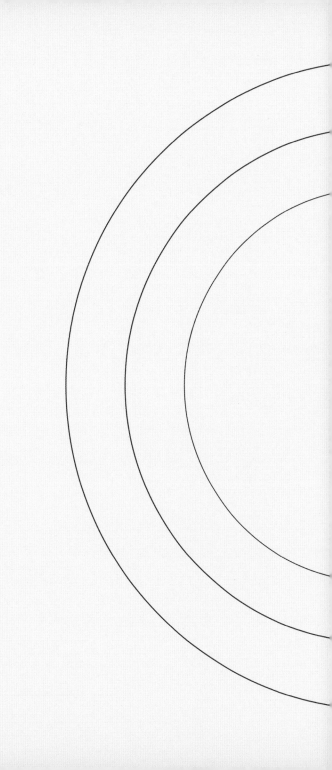

Reflection

Take a moment to explore how racial microaggressions make you feel.

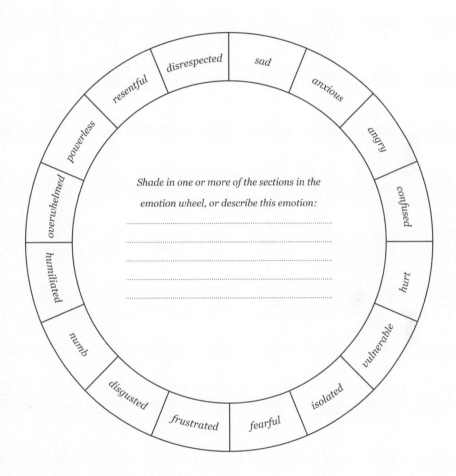

Shade in one or more of the sections in the emotion wheel, or describe this emotion:

disrespected · sad · anxious · angry · confused · hurt · vulnerable · isolated · fearful · frustrated · disgusted · numb · humiliated · overwhelmed · powerless · resentful

Reflect on a common negative message you receive about your racial identity. What goes through your mind when you receive this message?

....

....

....

What are some ways you can protect yourself from internalizing this message and others like it?

....

....

....

....

....

....

....

....

....

....

....

....

....

....

....

....

....

If you find yourself experiencing a racial microaggression, repeat these affirmations:

I have been worthy from the moment I was born.

I attract interactions that are full of love, respect, and support.

I reject any messages that tell me that I am unlovable or less valuable.

TENDER REMINDER

The _intent_ behind a message does not negate the _impact_ of the message. You deserve to be respected, affirmed, and loved always.

Returning
to Yourself

EXPLORING RACIAL OTHERING

Racial othering is when white people are treated as the norm, while Black, Indigenous, and people of color are treated as "different." It stems from a phenomenon called the *white default*, which defines white people as the standard for behavior, appearance, and culture.

Racial othering often takes place in the following ways:

- It defines white people as the default.
- It constructs and ascribes racial identities to BIPOC.
- It determines that this very racialization makes communities of color inferior.

During this process, communities of color are made to racially assimilate—to release our own ancestral practices, values, languages, food, clothing, appearance, and identities to fit in.

Racial assimilation is often talked about as a process that can be forced or voluntary. *Forced assimilation* refers to colonization, cultural genocide, slavery, and immigration policies that *coerce* us to conform to white culture. *Voluntary assimilation* refers to the idea that we *choose* to conform to white culture. But in a culture that conditions us to view whiteness as a symbol of superiority and privilege, racial assimilation is *never a choice*—it is always overtly or covertly forced.

If we are changing the most sacred parts of ourselves so that we can survive, assimilation cannot be considered voluntary. I can't help but think back to my youth, where the racial othering I experienced often made me question and swallow parts of my identity. The opposite of othering is belonging, and at our core, we all want to belong. However, we must constantly remind ourselves that belonging shouldn't leave us longing for ourselves.

RACIAL OTHERING

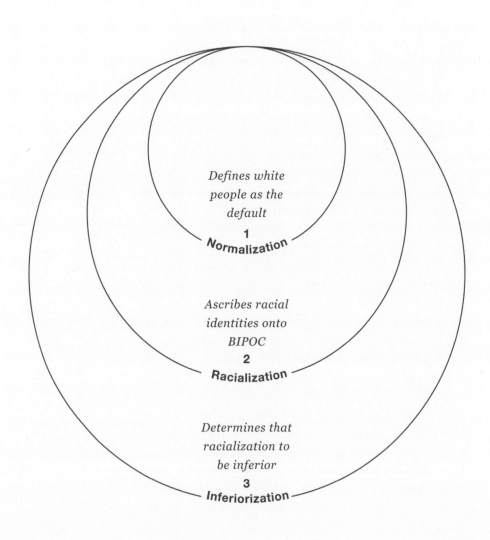

*Defines white
people as the
default*
**1
Normalization**

*Ascribes racial
identities onto
BIPOC*
**2
Racialization**

*Determines that
racialization to
be inferior*
**3
Inferiorization**

HOW RACIAL OTHERING MANIFESTS

Racial othering shows up in overt or covert ways, and it manifests as a normalization of whiteness, followed by the racialization and inferiorization of Black, Indigenous, and people of color.

Here's what these forms of racial othering look like:

NORMALIZATION OF WHITENESS

- *Creating media that only centers on white people and their experiences*
- *Teaching students solely about white experiences, culture, and history*
- *Creating codes of conduct about professionalism that adhere to white culture and condemn other cultures*
- *Viewing white people as the measure of success, intelligence, and accomplishment*
- *Designing products such as Band-Aids, coloring pencils, and cosmetics that come only in light tones*

RACIALIZATION OF BLACK, INDIGENOUS, AND PEOPLE OF COLOR

- *Calling BIPOC "diverse" or "different"*
- *Asking BIPOC, "Where are you really from?"*
- *Exotifying, fetishizing, or culturally appropriating BIPOC*
- *Calling nonwhite immigrants "illegals" or "aliens"*
- *Using comparative phrases such as "too Black" or "too Asian"*

INFERIORIZATION OF BLACK, INDIGENOUS, AND PEOPLE OF COLOR

- *Calling BIPOC "minorities"*
- *Saying "You people . . ." to refer to BIPOC*
- *Telling BIPOC who are talking in their native language to "speak English"*
- *Mocking the accents, food, mannerisms, dress, or languages of BIPOC*
- *Denying job interviews to people with non-Eurocentric names*

THE IMPACT OF RACIAL OTHERING

Here are some of the ways racial othering can impact you:

- It can lead to a loss of identity and feelings of homesickness.
- It can lead to feelings of shame and inferiority about your racial identity.
- It can cause you to police people in your community for not adhering to whiteness.
- It can cause you to distance yourself from people in your community.
- It can cause you to code-switch, which is when BIPOC shift their behavior, speech, and mannerisms to accommodate white values and norms.

Racial othering can cause Black, Indigenous, and people of color to participate in *respectability politics*. This is a phenomenon where we seek to create a connection with whiteness to counter negative perceptions about us and to gain respect, acceptance, and equal treatment from white people. We may conform to white standards of speech, dress, beauty, values, and behavior as a way of trying to prove that we are deserving of respect. However, respectability politics does not challenge racial othering; it simply perpetuates the idea that our worthiness is measured by how close we can get to whiteness. As we heal, we must remind ourselves that we don't belong to *whiteness*, we belong to *wholeness*.

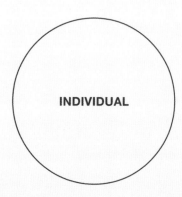

INDIVIDUAL

**HOW TO TEND
TO YOURSELF**

Affirm Your Identity

Continuous affirmation in the face of othering is an incredibly helpful way to come home to ourselves. Practice affirming your racial and cultural identity by doing the following:

- Watch, read, and engage with media that celebrates your racial identity and decenters whiteness.
- Seek out places, experiences, and people that honor your identity and allow you to be your whole self.
- Work with a decolonial guide or take a decolonial course that helps you unlearn colonial mindsets and reclaim who you are.

Racial Wellness

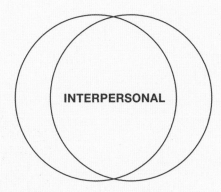

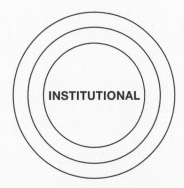

Challenge the White Default

When you notice or experience racial othering, it can be helpful to challenge the assumptions about who is "normal." Here is how you can do this:

- Challenge people who view white people as the image of success.
- If a person says someone is *"too* Black" or *"too* dark," ask them, "In comparison to who?"
- If someone says that you have a "funny/ strange" accent, remind them that everyone has an accent, including white people.
- Ask people, "Where are *you* really from?" after they ask you or another BIPOC that same question.

Advocate for Multiculturalism

Advocate for more awareness about the ways of being and living that aren't tied to whiteness. Here is how you can do this:

- Advocate for increased media such as books, television, and movies by decolonized BIPOC storytellers that convey the authentic stories and experiences of BIPOC to help challenge the idea that white is the norm.
- Encourage educational institutions to create mandatory decolonized curricu- lums and initiatives that highlight and celebrate a variety of cultures and lifestyles.

Reflection

Take a moment to explore how racial othering makes you feel.

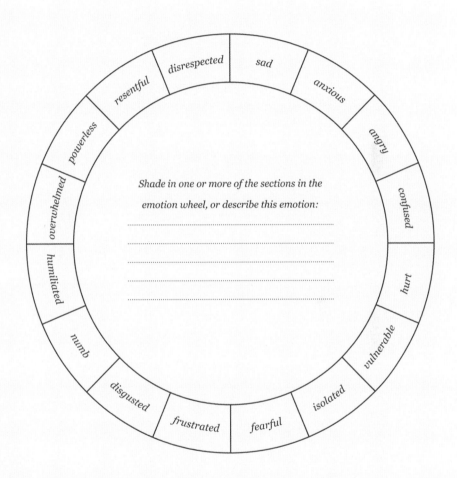

disrespected

sad

resentful

anxious

powerless

angry

overwhelmed

confused

Shade in one or more of the sections in the
emotion wheel, or describe this emotion:

....

....

....

....

....

humiliated

hurt

numb

vulnerable

disgusted

isolated

frustrated

fearful

Reflect on a time when you were racially othered. How did it impact your relationship with your racial identity?

....
....
....
....
....

Racial othering often makes us give up parts of ourselves. What are some ways that you would like to call these parts back into your life?

....
....
....
....
....
....
....
....
....
....
....
....
....
....
....
....

When you find yourself being othered, repeat these affirmations:

There are places I will go where I already belong.

I choose to accept myself and not abandon myself.

If it requires me to hide parts of myself to fit in, it's not for me.

TENDER REMINDER

You bring
yourself closer to
the wholeness your
ancestors wanted
you to experience by
reclaiming who you
were before
you were made
to forget.

A Love Note

ON ALIGNMENT

When we're constantly told that who we are at our core is wrong, it can make us feel like we should no longer sit in our skin. Many of us have shape-shifted so we can survive white supremacist culture. However, it is impossible to shape-shift without mis-aligning integral parts of ourselves.

Experiencing racism disconnects us from ourselves, from our community, and from our ancestors. As we hide parts of ourselves to fit in, we move further away from wholeness. And while external acceptance is not worth the spiritual cost of internal abandonment, being authentic to our true selves is not easy in a world that has often made it unsafe for us to do so.

My wish for us is that we find meaningful ways to come home to ourselves. I cultivate authenticity in my life by honoring my decolonial values, surrounding myself with Afrocentric art, revisiting ancestral stories, listening to Afrobeat, learning about my history, attending events that celebrate my ancestry, surrounding myself with people who welcome my full identity, and distancing myself from those who do not.

If you feel called to, take a moment to reflect on what being in alignment looks, feels, and sounds like to you.

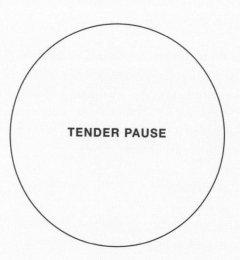

TENDER PAUSE

Take a break, breathe, and tend to <u>your spirit</u> before moving on to the next section of this racial wellness journey.

Interconnected Wellness

The previous chapters explored the ways in which racism can be traumatic to experience firsthand. However, a topic that is often overlooked in conversations about racism and trauma are the ways in which we can also experience secondhand racism, otherwise known as vicarious racism. This last chapter explores how to navigate this form of harm so that we can protect our peace.

Protecting Your Peace

EXPLORING VICARIOUS RACISM

Vicarious trauma speaks to instances when someone other than the direct victim experiences or witnesses abuse taking place. When Black, Indigenous, and people of color witness others experiencing racism, we often get secondary trauma in the form of vicarious racism.

While it is an overlooked form of racism, psychologist Shelly P. Harrell states that one of the six primary ways communities of color experience racism-related stress is through observing and learning about how other people experience racism. Vicarious racism makes us anxious about how we, our loved ones, and our community at large may experience the harm we witnessed. And yet, because people do not view racism as a form of abuse, they often fail to see how resurfacing incidents of racism can be deeply triggering, particularly if not done *with care*.

I vividly remember sitting in a class in high school where a white teacher was highlighting racist incidents that took place in history. In reenacting one particular incident, the teacher took on the role of the person who had committed the racist act and screamed out the N-word. My stomach dropped. I felt stunned, humiliated, and triggered. I was disturbed that this teacher had not only reenacted the incident without using a sensitivity warning, but that they had also used a violent, derogatory racial slur that non-Black people should never use.

What this teacher did not realize was that risking traumatizing me to educate white people about racism only reinforced my dehumanization. This is the danger of vicarious racism. People often feel that just because Black, Indigenous, and people of color may not be directly experiencing the racist incident *at that moment*, carelessly resurfacing incidents of racism doesn't hurt us. But our racial pain is deeply interconnected.

VICARIOUS RACISM

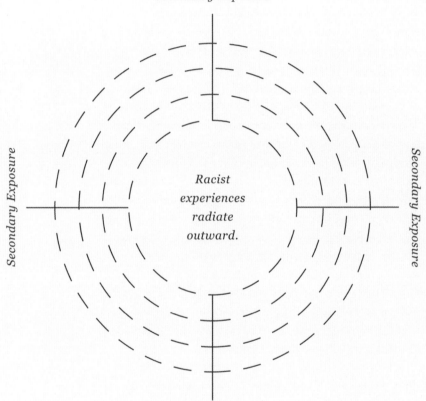

Secondary Exposure

Secondary Exposure

Secondary Exposure

Secondary Exposure

Racist experiences radiate outward.

HOW VICARIOUS RACISM MANIFESTS

Vicarious racism can be triggered by observing racist incidents, learning about them, and in some cases, having to recount them. This is particularly important in this digital age, where the scale and frequency on which racist incidents are publicized are unprecedented. With the virality of articles, videos, and images of racial harm, many of us are forced to repeatedly relive experiences of racism, often without warning.

Here is how vicarious racism can be triggered:

OBSERVING RACIST INCIDENTS

- *Witnessing other people experience racism, including police brutality, racial profiling, or racial violence*
- *Hearing racist rhetoric from public figures*
- *Seeing racist posts or posts that perpetuate harmful stereotypes about BIPOC on social media*

LEARNING ABOUT RACIST INCIDENTS

- *The media excessively distributing graphic images of racial harm*
- *Watching traumatic movies or documentaries about racist incidents*
- *Being taught about people's experiences with racism in a careless or offensive manner*

RECOUNTING RACIST INCIDENTS

- *Being asked to educate someone about racism or a racist incident*
- *Being asked triggering questions about racism or racist incidents*
- *Being asked to reenact a racist incident that took place, whether presently or in history*

THE IMPACT OF VICARIOUS RACISM

Here are some of the ways that vicarious racism can impact you:

- It can lead to depression, anxiety, and stress.
- It can make you feel dissociated and detached.
- It can lead to sleeplessness and difficulty falling asleep.
- It can cause you to have intrusive recurring thoughts of racist incidents.
- It can lead you to be hypervigilant for your safety, that of your loved ones, and that of those in your community.

Continuously witnessing other people in our communities experience racism can lead to harmful health consequences. When Black, Indigenous, and people of color experience vicarious racism, it reminds us that we are also vulnerable to the racism that we have learned about or witnessed. While it is difficult for us to escape racism in the world we currently live in, there are moments when we can set boundaries that give us a feeling of relief from the trauma.

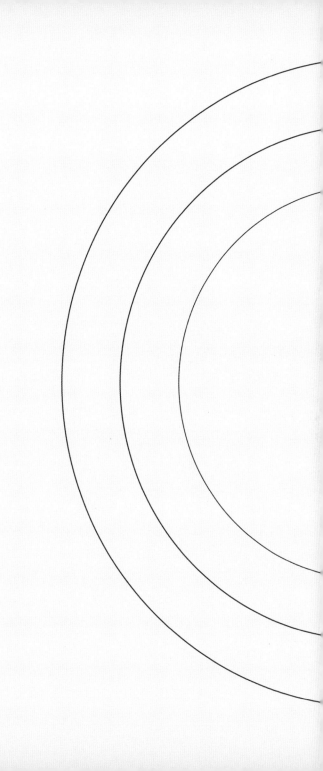

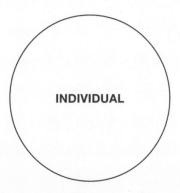

INDIVIDUAL

HOW TO TEND TO YOURSELF

Create a Coping Ritual

Create rituals to help you navigate vicarious racism. Here is what that can look like:

- Log out of social media when people are posting about racist incidents.
- Take breaks from watching or reading the news about racist incidents.
- Take time off from work or school, if possible, to pour into yourself.
- Seek support from a healing practitioner who understands your experiences.
- Go out into nature to help ground yourself.

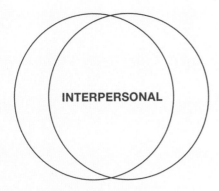

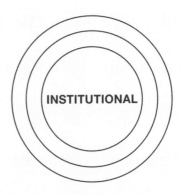

Assert Your Boundaries

When you don't have the capacity to engage in racially triggering conversations, try asserting the following boundaries:

- "Please be mindful that it can be triggering to hear this as someone with lived experience."
- "In the future, could you add a content warning before posting racially traumatic content?"
- "In the future, please do not send me this type of news because it triggers me."
- "I do not have the capacity to educate you about this, but there are great online resources you can consult."
- "I'm not in the right space to hear about or talk about this right now. Could we revisit the subject later?"

Champion Trauma-Informed Care

Advocate for institutions to become trauma-informed so they can better care for people who experience vicarious racism. You can ask your school or workplace to do the following:

- Acknowledge traumatic instances of racism.
- Recognize how these events impact the mental and emotional health of BIPOC.
- Provide healing services, safe spaces, and time off for individuals experiencing trauma.
- Ensure that when people engage with BIPOC about racial abuse, they ask for consent, use considerate language, and provide sensitivity warnings before sharing race-based content.

Reflection

Take a moment to explore how vicarious racism makes you feel.

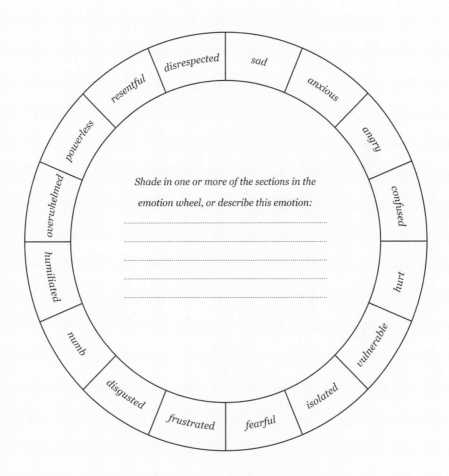

Shade in one or more of the sections in the emotion wheel, or describe this emotion:

....

....

....

....

disrespected · *sad* · *anxious* · *angry* · *confused* · *hurt* · *vulnerable* · *isolated* · *fearful* · *frustrated* · *disgusted* · *numb* · *humiliated* · *overwhelmed* · *powerless* · *resentful*

Reflect on a time when you witnessed a racially traumatic image or video. What went through your mind?

....

....

....

....

....

What are some boundaries that you can set to reduce the vicarious trauma you experience?

....

....

....

....

....

....

....

....

....

....

....

....

....

....

....

....

....

....

....

When you find yourself about to engage in a conversation or with media that may lead to vicarious racial trauma, repeat these affirmations:

I deserve to set boundaries to support my racial well-being.

I can take breaks from reliving traumatic racist experiences.

I don't need to engage in racially traumatic conversations or media to know that racism is alive.

TENDER REMINDER

You were not designed to continuously breathe in trauma. You deserve the space to heal from the racial harm we collectively experience.

Postlude

A significant reason why I wrote this book is to provide Black, Indigenous, and people of color with the language to express the forms of racism that we hear, see, and feel in so many aspects of our lives. When we lack the language around concepts such as racial gaslighting, racial fear, or racial apathy, it makes it all the more difficult for us to identify, articulate, and resist the harm we experience.

When you give abuse a name, you bring it out from its hiding place. You're able to observe it, analyze it, and explore how to disempower it. I have often found that when I have the terminology to describe a form of abuse that I've experienced, it makes it easier for me to process it. In naming the abuse, I find clarity. In naming the abuse, I find validation. In naming the abuse, I find possibility. Possibility to heal.

I recall walking through a museum and coming across a quote by artist Lhola Amira that stopped me in my tracks: "Where does it hurt, why does it hurt, how does it hurt, and what do WE do with our wounded-ness? How can WE move through the wound and gesture for healing?" My hope is that all that has been articulated on these pages will help you answer these questions, and reimagine what it means to birth a world that cultivates racial wellness for your ancestors, yourself, and the generations that may follow you.

As people who have experienced racial oppression, creating a healthy legacy is a form of alchemy. Some of the racial trauma that we carry in our bodies is from those who came before us, and it can be passed down to those who may come after us. This is called *intergenerational trauma*. It is essentially an embodied memory from someone in your lineage about the pain they experienced.

Intergenerational trauma is made possible through *epigenetics*, which is the study of how our environment can influence the way our genes work. Epigenetics teaches us that living in a racially traumatic environment can actually *alter* our genes. These altered genes contain the biological memory of the trauma we endured and can be passed down to future generations. This trauma may manifest as stress, anxiety, insomnia, nightmares, and more. And while this is a heavy burden to carry, I want it to be known that epigenetics works *both ways*. Living in racially healed environments can also alter our genes for the *better*.

Our legacy of healing is dependent on the worlds we build. This is why I believe that unpacking racial trauma and integrating racial wellness tools into our emotional, mental, physical, and spiritual lives on individual, interpersonal, and institutional levels is so vital. When we create intentional strategies that help us respond to our racial wounds while also working to dismantle the cause of these racial wounds, we open up the possibilities for healing.

May we unravel
worlds that oppress
us and weave worlds
that free us.

More
Tenderness

I want to take a moment to highlight some visionaries, resources, and explorations that can help support your racial wellness journey. May we lean on all the collective tenderness we have so that we can become free.

VISIONARIES

These are writers, activists, healers, artists, researchers, abolitionists, and organizers whose work is a constant reminder that liberation is our birthright.

Maya Angelou

Ella Baker

James Baldwin

Steve Biko

adrienne maree brown

Thema Bryant

Mariel Buqué

Robert T. Carter

Lillian Comas-Díaz

Angela Davis

Joy DeGruy

Frantz Fanon

Natalie Y. Gutiérrez

Annika Hansteen-Izora

Tricia Hersey (The Nap Bishop)

bell hooks

Ji-Youn Kim

Sahaj Kaur Kohli

Audre Lorde

Alyssa Mancao (Alyssa Marie Wellness)

Alishia McCullough

Resmaa Menakem

Toni Morrison

Jennifer Mullan

Rocío Rosales Meza

Gabes Torres

Nayyirah Waheed

Malcolm X

RESOURCES

These are healing resources that can support you as you move through your racial wellness journey.

Alkeme Health

| AlkemeHealth.com

Asian Mental Health Collective

| AsianMHC.org

Ayana Therapy

| AyanaTherapy.com

Brown Girl Therapy

| Instagram.com/BrownGirlTherapy

Cultural Somatics Institute

| CulturalSomaticsInstitute.com

Decolonizing Therapy

| Instagram.com/DecolonizingTherapy

Inclusive Therapists

| InclusiveTherapists.com

Indigenous Circle of Wellness

| ICOWellness.com

Latinx Therapy

| LatinxTherapy.com

Making the Body a Home

| MakingTheBodyAHome.co

Melanin and Mental Health

| MelaninAndMentalHealth.com

South Asian Mental Health Initiative and Network

| SAMHIN.org

The Nap Ministry

| TheNapMinistry.com

Therapy for Black Girls

| TherapyForBlackGirls.com

Therapy for Black Men

| TherapyForBlackMen.org

Therapy for Latinx

| TherapyForLatinx.com

Therapy for Queer People of Color

| TherapyForQPOC.com

Therapy in Color

| TherapyInColor.org

EXPLORATIONS

These books, essays, articles, and research papers can help you learn more about the paradigms explored in each section of this book.

PRELUDE

- "Racism and Psychological and Emotional Injury: Recognizing and Assessing Race-Based Traumatic Stress" by Robert T. Carter; *The Counseling Psychologist*, volume 35, no. 1, January 2007, https://doi.org/10.1177/0011000006292033.
- "Racist Incident-Based Trauma" by Thema Bryant-Davis and Carlota Ocampo; *The Counseling Psychologist*, volume 33, no. 4, July 2005, https://doi.org/10.1177/0011000005276465.
- "Racial Trauma: Theory, Research, and Healing: Introduction to the Special Issue" by Lillian Comas-Díaz, Gordon Nagayama Hall, and Helen A. Neville; *American Psychologist*, volume 74, no. 1, January 2019, http://dx.doi.org/10.1037/amp0000442.
- "The Four Bodies: A Holistic Toolkit for Coping with Racial Trauma" by Jacquelyn Ogorchukwu Iyamah; *Medium.com*, May 30, 2020, https://medium.com/nappy-head-club/the-four-bodies-a-holistic -toolkit-for-coping-with-racial-trauma-8d15aa55ae06.

INTERLUDE

- "Endless Mourning: Racial Melancholia, Black Grief, and the Transformative Possibilities for Racial Justice in Education" by Justin Grinage; *Harvard Educational Review*, volume 89, no. 2, Summer 2019, https://doi.org/10.17763/1943–5045–89.2.227.

EMOTIONAL WELLNESS

- "How the Ukraine Crisis Reveals Our Racial Empathy Gap" by Ainsley Hawthorn; *CBC Opinion*, March 12, 2022, https://www .cbc.ca/news/canada/newfoundland-labrador/how-the-ukraine -crisis-reveals-our-racial-empathy-gap-1.6380344.
- *Feeling Power: Emotions and Education* by Megan Boler; Routledge, 1999.

- *Tenderness: An Honoring of My Black Queer Joy and Rage* by Annika Hansteen-Izora; Co-Conspirator Press, 2021.
- *My Grandmother's Hands: Racialized Trauma and the Pathway to Mending Our Hearts and Bodies* by Resmaa Menakem; Central Recovery Press, 2017.
- "The Effects of Racial Profiling" by the Ontario Human Rights Commission; https://www.ohrc.on.ca/en/paying-price-human -cost-racial-profiling/effects-racial-profiling.
- "Just Walk on By: Black Men and Public Space" by Brent Staples; *Harper's*, 1987, https://www.yumpu.com/en/document/view /34010593/just-walk-on-by-black-men-and-public-space -fogccsfedu.

MENTAL WELLNESS

- "Racial Gaslighting" by Angelique M. Davis and Rose Ernst; *Politics, Groups, and Identities*, volume 7, no. 4, 2019, https://doi .org/10.1080/21565503.2017.1403934.
- "This Woman's Post About Racial Gaslighting Blew Up Online— Here's Why It's Important" by Liz Richardson; *BuzzFeed*, June 9, 2020, https://www.buzzfeed.com/lizmrichardson/racial-gaslighting -instagram-explainer.
- "Violations of Power, Adaptive Blindness, and Betrayal Trauma Theory" by Jennifer J. Freyd; *Feminism & Psychology*, volume 7, no. 1, February 1997, http://dx.doi.org/10.1177/095935359707 1004.
- "The Racial Triangulation of Asian Americans" by Claire Jean Kim; *Politics & Society*, volume 27, no. 1, March 1999, https://doi.org /10.1177/0032329299027001005.
- "Framing Asian Suffering in an Anti-Black World: A Conversation with Claire Jean Kim" by Weishun Lu; *EdgeEffects,* September 23, 2021, https://edgeeffects.net/claire-jean-kim.
- "Hate Crimes Against Asian Americans" by Yan Zhang, Lening Zhang, and Francis Benton; *American Journal of Criminal Justice,* volume 47, January 7, 2021, http://dx.doi.org/10.1007/s12103 –020–09602–9.

- *The Master's Tools Will Never Dismantle the Master's House* by Audre Lorde; Penguin UK, 2018.

PHYSICAL WELLNESS

- "'Every Shut Eye, Ain't Sleep': The Role of Racism-Related Vigilance in Racial/Ethnic Disparities in Sleep Difficulty" by Margaret T. Hicken et al.; *Race and Social Problems*, volume 5, June 2013, http://dx.doi.org/10.1007/s12552–013–9095–9.
- "Socioeconomic Status, John Henryism, and Hypertension in Blacks and Whites" by Sherman A. James et al.; *American Journal of Epidemiology*, volume 126, no. 4, October 1987, https://doi.org/10.1093/oxfordjournals.aje.a114706.
- "'Weathering' and Age Patterns of Allostatic Load Scores Among Blacks and Whites in the United States" by Arline T. Geronimus et al.; *American Journal of Public Health*, volume 96, 2006, http://dx .doi.org/10.2105/AJPH.2004.060749.
- "John Henryism and the Health of African-Americans" by Sherman A. James; *Culture, Medicine and Psychiatry,* volume 18, no. 2, 1994, http://hdl.handle.net/2027.42/45356.
- "Resistance and Resilience: The Sojourner Syndrome and the Social Context of Reproduction in Central Harlem" by Leith Mullings; *Transforming Anthropology*, January 2008, http://dx.doi .org/10.1525/tran.2005.13.2.79.

SPIRITUAL WELLNESS

- "Offensive Mechanisms" by Chester D. Pierce; *The Black Seventies,* Porter Sargent, 1970, https://dokumen.tips/documents /offensive-mechanisms-chester-pierce.html.
- "Racial Microaggressions in Everyday Life: Implications for Clinical Practice" by Derald Wing Sue et al.; *American Psychologist*, volume 62, no. 4, May 2007, http://dx.doi.org/10.1037/0003 –066X.62.4.271.
- *Microintervention Strategies: What You Can Do to Disarm and Dismantle Individual and Systemic Racism and Bias* by Derald

Wing Sue et al.; John Wiley & Sons, 2021.

- "Racial Battle Fatigue and the MisEducation of Black Men: Racial Microaggressions, Societal Problems, and Environmental Stress" by William A. Smith, Man Hung, and Jeremy D. Franklin; *The Journal of Negro Education*, volume 80, no. 1, Winter 2011, https://www.jstor.org/stable/41341106.
- "What Is Cultural Assimilation?" by Zuva Seven; *Verywell Mind*, updated June 27, 2022, https://www.verywellmind.com/what-is -cultural-assimilation-5225960.
- "Understanding Respectability Politics" by Emily Chen and Jenny Dorsey; *Studio ATAO*, updated July 1, 2021, https://www .studioatao.org/respectability-politics.

OUR INTERCONNECTED WELLNESS

- "A Multidimensional Conceptualization of Racism-Related Stress: Implications for the Well-Being of People of Color" by Shelly P. Harrell; *American Journal of Orthopsychiatry*, volume 70, no. 1, February 2000, http://dx.doi.org/10.1037/h0087722.

POSTLUDE

- *Facing the Future* by Lhola Amira; de Young Museum, 2022, https://www.famsf.org/exhibitions/lhola-amira.
- *Post Traumatic Slave Syndrome: America's Legacy of Enduring Injury and Healing* by Joy DeGruy; Joy DeGruy Publications, 2017.
- "The Intergenerational Impact of Racism on Health" by Shamard Charles; *Verywell Health*, updated August 1, 2022, https://www .verywellhealth.com/intergenerational-impact-of-racism-on-health -5076155.
- "The Transgenerational Consequences of Discrimination on African-American Health Outcomes" by Bridget J. Goosby and Chelsea Heidbrink; *Sociology Compass*, volume 7, no. 8, August 2013, http://dx.doi.org/10.1111/soc4.12054.

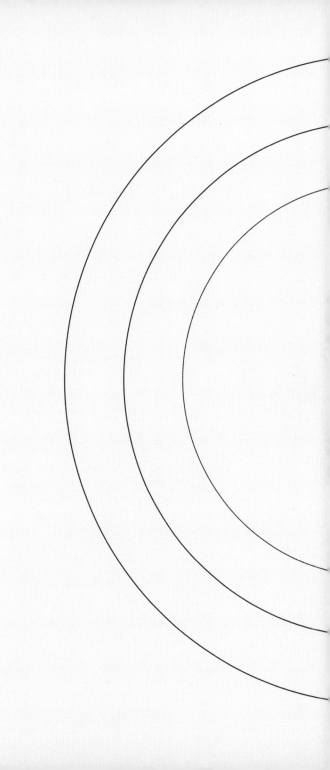

Gratitude

This book would not have been possible without the beautiful people who have touched my life in ways I could have never imagined.

TO MY FAMILY, thank you for *inspiring* me. You showed me how to put my all into the things that matter. **TO MY FRIENDS,** thank you for *encouraging* me. It has been a blessing to have you in my life as a soft landing place. **TO MY MENTORS,** thank you for *guiding* me. You gave me the space to deeply unpack the dynamics of white supremacy. **TO MY BIPOC COMMUNITY,** thank you for *resonating* with me. Your vulnerability has been a sacred reminder of how important this work is. **TO KATE,** my literary agent, thank you for *honoring* me. Throughout this process, you helped me to constantly remember my worth. **TO SAHARA,** my editor, thank you for *seeing* the love I'm trying to put out into the world. You pushed me to breathe life into this vision. **TO SAULT,** thank you for *invigorating* me. I wrote the majority of this book listening to your song "Free."

Here's to dreaming, designing, and developing new worlds that make us feel free.

About
the Author

Jacquelyn Ogorchukwu Iyamah (she/her) is the designer, writer, and cultural worker behind the term *racial wellness*. She is the founder of Making the Body a Home, where she designs home goods, decor, and courses that help people stimulate racial wellness within their interior spaces.

She has a bachelor's degree in social welfare from the University of California, Berkeley, where her focus was on researching the societal factors that impact the well-being of communities of color. She also has a master's degree in science in interaction design, where her thesis focused on designing spaces for communities of color to heal. She taps into theory from her social welfare degree, praxis from her interaction design degree, and wisdom from her loving ancestors to reimagine the ways in which racial healing can take place.

Visit MakingTheBodyAHome.co to learn more about her work.